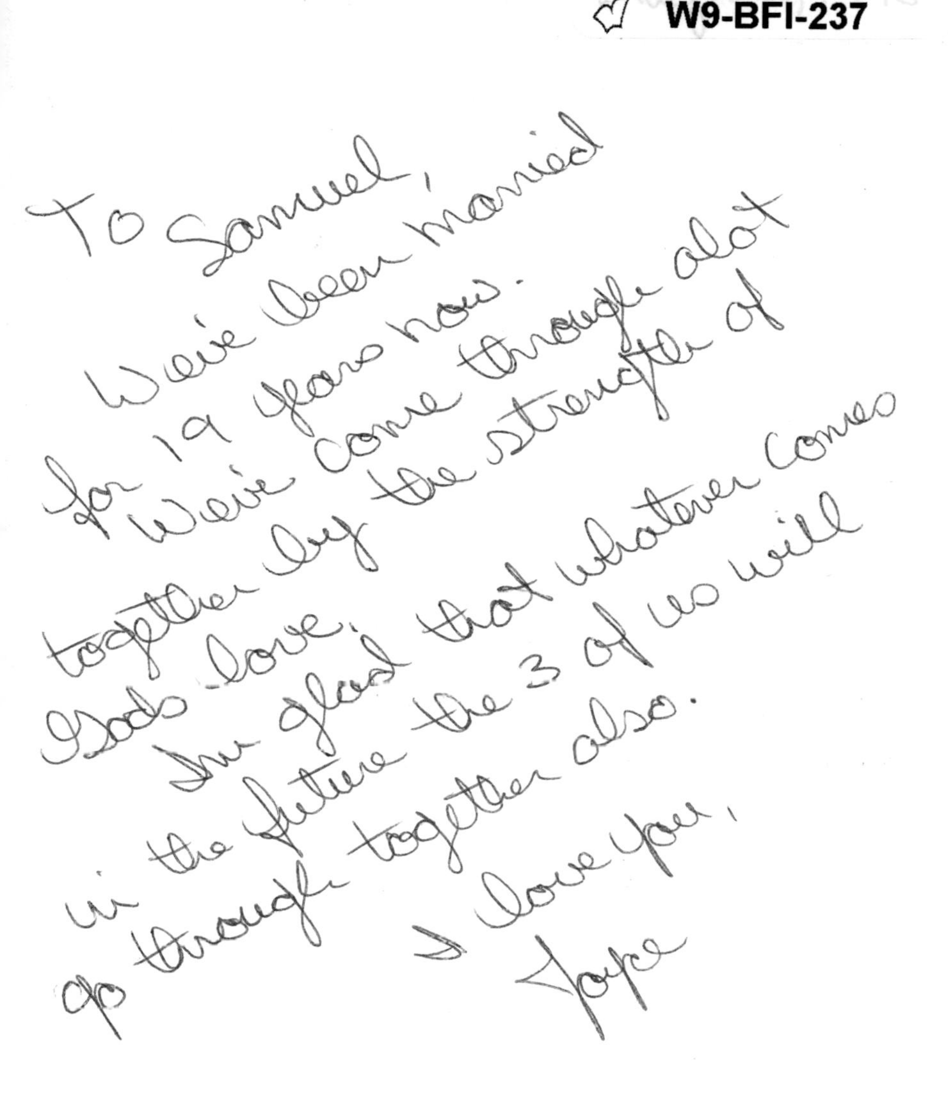

To Samuel,
We've been married for 19 years now.
We've come through alot together by the strength of Gods love.
I'm glad that whatever comes in the future the 3 of us will go through together also.
I love you,
Joyce

"Ours is a nation of families who are exhausted from haste. But, life is ***not*** a 100-yard dash, it's a marathon. Pace is more important than haste. Russ Crosson offers a perspective of remarkable clarity and simplicity that will give your family pace for your race."

Steve Farrar
President, Point Man Leadership Ministries

"This book will challenge your thinking. It makes a significant contribution toward understanding the biblical perspective of money and possessions. I pray it will stimulate you to become financially faithful."

Howard Dayton
President, Crown Ministries

"This book is a much needed antidote to unbiblical thinking regarding finances. Russ Crosson's emphasis on 'posterity' rather than 'prosperity' and eternal rather than temporal investments, if applied, will make you eternally grateful."

Walter A. Henrichsen
Author

"This book captures key biblical insights in the area of our prosperity. And it comes from a man who 'walks the talk.' Russ Crosson meets the challenge of fair-mindedness and readiness mentioned in Acts 17:11. Here is a book for us to learn from."

Gayle M. Jackson
President, CAD Systems, Inc.

"Although this book offers a wealth of practical financial advice, it takes a significant step beyond the 'how to's' of money management to answer the more vital 'why' questions. I have seen Russ Crosson consistently model these truths in his own life and have witnessed their impact in the lives of others, including me!"

Tim Kallam
Pastor, Fellowship Bible Church
Roswell, GA

"Russ Crosson always keeps the big picture in mind when it comes to money. He reminds us to look at money from an eternal, lifelong perspective. That's why this book is a key to *A Life Well Spent.*"

Bryant Wright
Senior Pastor, Johnson Ferry Baptist Church
Atlanta, GA

"Russ Crosson does an excellent job of taking us back to the basics, not only of finance, but how to integrate important principles into our total life system."

Colonel Nimrod McNair
President, McNair Associates, Inc.

To Clark, Reed, and Chad, my posterity, whom I pray will manifest the truths shared in this book and pass them on to the generations that come after them to the glory of God.

A Life Well Spent

RUSS CROSSON

THOMAS NELSON PUBLISHERS
Nashville • Atlanta • London • Vancouver

Published in Nashville, Tennessee, by Thomas Nelson, Inc., Publishers, and distributed in Canada by Word Communications, Ltd., Richmond, British Columbia.

Many of the anecdotes in this volume are based on fact; however, names and details have been changed to protect identities.

Library of Congress Cataloging-in-Publication Data

Crosson, Russ, 1953–
A life well spent : the eternal rewards of investing yourself and your money in your family / Russ Crosson.
p. cm.
Includes bibliographical references.
ISBN 0-7852-8015-4
1. Finance, Personal—Religious aspects—Christianity. 2. Wealth—Religious aspects—Christianity. 3. Christian giving. 4. Family—Religious life. I. Title.
HG179.C75 1994
332.024—dc20 94-26037
CIP

Printed in the United States of America
1 2 3 4 5 6 7 — 98 97 96 95 94

Contents

ACKNOWLEDGMENTS

As with any such undertaking, this book would have been impossible without the assistance and encouragement of countless people. Most important, I am grateful to Julie, my wife of fifteen years, who is a constant source of encouragement to me. Without her unwavering love, support, and devotion, and her continual training and teaching of our children, the concepts shared in this book would only be hollow words with no substance.

I also owe a debt of gratitude to my partners at Ronald Blue and Company. First and foremost, to Ron Blue, the managing partner, for allowing me the time to work on this project. Second, to my other partners from whom many of the insights in this book were gained. A very special thanks goes to Chip Vaughan, Curt Knorr, Angie Wells, Barry Vaughan, and Bert Harned for their detailed reading and analysis of the initial manuscript. Their thoughts, comments, and input, contained throughout these pages, were invaluable in developing this final product.

I am also grateful to Mike Hyatt and Robert Wolgemuth for their encouragement and for representing me throughout this process. It was their comments early in the process that gave me the strength to see this project through to completion. My editor, Janet Thoma, was instrumental in putting the final touches on the manuscript.

Karen Vaughan, my long-time administrative assistant, deserves a special commendation for her countless hours of typing and editing while responding to many other demands as this book was being developed. Now that Karen has been promoted to a new position with

Ronald Blue and Company, Mary Schmidt is to be thanked for picking up where Karen left off, assisting in the completion of this book.

Finally, I thank the Wednesday-morning men's Bible study group in which I participate for their prayers and encouragement through this process.

Foreword

All Christians who are sincere in their faith long to stand before the Lord and hear Him say, "Well done, good and faithful servant; you were faithful over a few things, I will make you ruler over many things. Enter into the joy of your Lord." *A Life Well Spent* is written by a person who has a passion like few I know to live his life in such a way as to hear those words.

Russ and I have worked together for the last fifteen years in building a financial planning practice that helps Christians integrate biblical principles of money and money management into a life and family. The reality is that when you make money decisions, you make life decisions. Money and other financial resources are scarce for all of us, no matter how much we possess. As a consequence, all money is allocated to the real priorities of life. We believe that money is a resource that God entrusts to us to be used in many different ways for the accomplishment of His plans and purposes. Ultimately, as those of us who are believers in the Lord Jesus Christ use the resources that He has entrusted to us, we act as salt and light in a world that desperately needs to see proper models of lives that are balanced and ultimately well spent.

Russ has done a masterful job of dealing with some of the tremendous challenges that people face in allocating their financial resources. For example, what is the trade-off between prosperity and posterity? This book answers that question in a way that is easy to understand but incredibly challenging to apply.

Believe me, you can trust the content of this book. It

is built on probably more experience than almost anyone in this country has had in counseling and consulting with couples and individuals in the area of money and money management. Russ understands very well the role that money plays in our lives.

You will find this book to be provocative, challenging, encouraging, practical, and, best of all, biblical. Russ Crosson is a man with a passion to share the practical outworkings of faith in the area of family and finances. I recommend this book without reservation.

Ron Blue

Part One

A Life Well Spent

1

A Glimpse of Eternity

A New Perspective on Money and Family

High up in the North, in the land called Svithjod, there stands a rock. It is 100 miles high and 100 miles wide. Once every 1,000 years a little bird comes to this rock to sharpen its beak. When the rock has thus been worn away, then a single day of eternity will have gone by.

Henry Willen Van Loon

In My Father's house are many mansions; if it were not so, I would have told you. I go to prepare a place for you. And if I go and prepare a place for you, I will come again and receive you to Myself; that where I am, there you may be also.

Jesus, speaking in John 14:2–3

It began as an uneventful Sunday morning. Jim had been calmly sitting in the third pew on the right-hand side of the Sunnydale Evangelical Church, a pew he and Barbara had warmed on and off for some twenty years. Pastor Firnbeck was preaching on rewards and eternity, his rich, vibrant voice filling the sanctuary as he recited 1 Corinthians 3:13–15: "Each one's work will become manifest; for the Day will declare it, because it will be revealed by fire; and the fire will test each one's work, of what sort it is. If anyone's work which he has built on it endures, he will receive a reward. If anyone's work is burned, he will suffer loss."

Jim's mind wandered as he pondered the Great Day when his turn for judgment would come and he would receive his reward. The words teased him to imagine vast riches: a mansion larger than the one he and Barbara occupied now, suits as well fitting as those his tailor made for him (but these would be pure silk), a Mercedes to replace the BMW . . .

The sharp pain seemed to hit shortly after the little smile creased his lips. It came out of nowhere—though Jim would later think it came right from heaven, a bolt of electricity so powerful it sucked every molecule of air from his lungs. *Pain*—a word he knew little about but became intimately acquainted with in one split second—hit his chest and riveted down his arm. He could not scream. He could not move. He was alert, awake, yet unable to speak. There was a flurry of motion—Barbara calling his name, the pastor rushing down from the podium, Mrs. Monroe's large hat flying up. The words *ambulance, doctor, heart attack* flew past his ears, yet still that electrical pain held him in its grip.

What followed could only be described as Reckoning Day. The ride in the ambulance, the panic that filled his very soul, the awareness that judgment was no longer a fantasy about a day in the future but something that might take place within the next moment.

The hospital staff was efficient and quick; the pain, relentless. Tubes of every shape and size invaded his body, whirring, hissing, menacing.

An hour passed. Jim heard his name and tried to open his eyes but could not find the strength. Then he recognized his son's voice. Jimmy's questions to the nurse were pointed, cold, and emotionless: "How much longer does he have?"

"I'm sorry, but we have done everything we can possibly do for him."

"Do I have to stay around the hospital or could you just call me when he's gone?"

"Just leave your number at the desk, sir, and we will call you when there is a change."

Brisk, abrupt, businesslike, and uncaring, Jimmy's footsteps led to the door. Then his voice came again, as he needed to explain: "I hardly know my dad. He was never home for us . . . always making a buck, always making a name. I . . . I . . . I'm sorry."

What do you mean I was never there for you! You lived in the biggest house in the neighborhood, didn't you? You drove the fanciest car of any kid in your high school, and didn't you spend a couple of months touring Europe in the twelfth grade at my expense? The silent argument screamed inside Jim's head. Then the anger turned to quiet but painful sobs that were lost to the whirring of the machines.

Time seemed shrouded in thick veils. Pastor Firnbeck was whispering above him. Barbara was there too; he could smell her rich perfume. She was crying. The minister was telling him the names of the twenty or so families who at that very moment were in the waiting room, praying for him. Those families marched before his mind's eye. Several had some serious needs over the past few years, but he had never felt led to help in any way;

he had been too busy. Pastor Firnbeck also talked of baskets of food already arriving at their home, of Joe Babcock flying his private plane to Philadelphia, three hundred miles away, to pick up Jim and Barbara's daughter, Jill, so she could get to the hospital as soon as possible. Jim remembered that Babcock had asked him to contribute to a medical piloting ministry just six months before, but Jim had thought it was a waste of money—money now being lavishly spent on him.

Then a strange voice filled the room—a voice of authority, confidence—calling for a drug, explaining to Barbara the purpose and the hope. Jim could feel the needle entering his arm, then warm fluid entered his body and his mind slowly lost its grip . . . going, going into twilight.

But this wasn't twilight. It was a waiting room. The carpet was red, royal red. Music (Was it piped in?) filled the room. Yet was it a room? Jim could not tell. He was sitting on a soft, comfortable sofa. Others were in the room, or so it seemed. He felt them, though he really couldn't focus on what they looked like.

"James Conwell." His name was being called, but he had no idea who was calling it. As he stood up, doors directly across from him opened, and he walked through. What met him was astounding. A room the size of . . . well, how could he even measure it? And it wasn't just the size. It was the awesome light. There was a throne. There was a robe, long and luxurious, filling up the entire room. There were strange creatures. Majesty and beauty. There was fear, and there was power. *There was God.* This was it . . . the Day . . . This was no fantasy . . . This was reality.

Moments, hours, or perhaps years passed in silence. Jim could not tell. He could not think; he could not speak. The words came from the throne. The voice was love. "Jim, it is time to test your life works," it said, booming—or was it whispering?—across the room. And then his life appeared: their first home, their first car (he had forgotten that little green Plymouth), the 457-page project he had spent a year working on with six other coworkers, another home, tennis courts, a swimming pool, a fishing boat, more cars, several exclusive clubs where they held memberships, twelve file cabinets full of papers—all his projects, his financial schemes, his investments—a summer home, a larger boat, his bank accounts . . . The pile grew and grew and grew.

Jim wondered how the room contained it all. He was awestruck by the impressive display of goods before him. *I am wealthy beyond imagination,* he could hear his inner voice telling him, cheering him on. *Rich at last, rich for all eternity,* he literally sang under his breath.

Then the voice came again . . . "And now, Jim, the test of fire!" Where the fire came from, Jim had no idea. Though he was standing near the enormous pile, he was neither warmed nor singed by the blaze. But the fire came, and in one moment all was gone. *All was gone!*

Jim recalled the words read just that morning by Pastor Firnbeck, "If anyone's work is burned, he will suffer loss." Sixty-one years of life, all for one small pile of ashes. Jim could feel it before he actually heard it: deep sobs coming from his soul, weakening his knees, breaking his strength, flattening him out as he realized he had lived and worked all of his life for nothing, absolutely nothing of lasting value.

"Mr. Conwell." His name again, this time from a different voice. *Where am I?* The sound of whirring machines, the smell of perfume, the feel of the gurney under him, the nurse, Pastor Firnbeck, tears on his cheeks. He awakened from the dream for one more chance . . .[1]

A New Perspective on Money and Family

As a partner in the financial and investment advisory firm of Ronald Blue and Company, I have observed the tensions between money and family at all the various stages of life: The young couple starts out and struggles with a budget, work pressures, and the demands of a growing family. The middle-aged corporate executive, entrepreneur, or doctor whose children are in their late teens begins to question whether his or her all-consuming work was worth it. The older couple approaches retirement and wonders what to do now.

These observations, as well as the current lack of "why-to" books in the marketplace, have burdened me to write this book. There are countless publications on financial planning, investments, debt, budgeting, and training your children but nothing that puts into context *why* one should be interested in all those areas. This book is written to fill that gap. It is designed to be a primer to the other financial books. On the one hand, this book is about money, but on the other hand, it is not about money at all. It is about money only in the context of something more important—your life and eternity.

Preparing for Eternity

To prepare for eternity, we must first have a keen awareness and a clear understanding that there will be a day of judgment for us. "And as it is appointed for men to die once, but after this the judgment" (Heb. 9:27). Many of us live as if there is no judgment, and as a result we act as if it really doesn't matter how we live, especially after we trust Christ as our Savior. This is a result, it seems, of an unclear perspective on the two distinct judgments mentioned in Scripture.

One concept of judgment has to do with our sin; we will be judged as to whether we have accepted Christ's payment for our sin and by faith have trusted Him to be our Savior. If we accept Christ as Savior, our names will be found in the Book of Life (see Rev. 20:12 and 15), we will enter into heaven (see John 1:12), and our sins will be remembered no more (see Heb. 10:17). If we have not personally trusted Christ, we will be cast into the lake of fire and will experience eternal separation from God (see Rev. 20:15). (Note: If you have never trusted Christ as your Savior, see Appendix A to learn how.)

The second concept of judgment, and the one that should affect how we live our lives as believers, has to do with the judgment of our works.

Just as Jim Conwell dreamed, we will one day "appear before the judgment seat of Christ" where our works will be tested "according to what [we have] done, whether good or bad" (2 Cor. 5:10). Salvation is by grace, not by works (see Eph. 2:8–9). However, this judgment is of our works and deeds, so it does matter how we live as believers. And since, unlike Jim, we do not get a second chance, our decisions today regarding money and family are critical in order to live effectively.

In God's plan the service of each of His children is scrutinized and evaluated (see Matt. 12:36; Rom. 14:10; Gal. 6:7; Eph. 6:8; and Col. 3:24–25). As a result of this judgment there will be a reward or a loss of reward to the believer, as Pastor Firnbeck read from 1 Corinthians 3.

You may be thinking, *What difference does it make whether I have reward or loss of reward if I'm in heaven?* Scripture indicates through use of phrases such as "more tolerable" (Matt. 11:20–24) or "greater condemnation" (Luke 20:45–47) that there are levels of judgment and reward. My position of rulership with Christ in heaven will be determined by how I live now. So it does matter how I live!

What are God's desires about how we live regarding our money and our family? There is only one place to find that out: in God's handbook for life, the Bible. John 17:17 says, "Your word is truth." And John 8:32 says, "You shall know the truth, and the truth shall make you free." What is important to God revolves around things that are eternal versus things that are temporal. "We do not look at the things which are seen, but at the things which are not seen. For the things which are seen are temporary, but the things which are not seen are eternal" (2 Cor. 4:18). *Temporal* means "to last for a limited time or to be transient or provisional." *Eternal* means "to be ceaseless, everlasting, or endless."

Once we understand that God is more concerned about the eternal than the temporal, we face some unique challenges in the financial area.

Once we understand that God is more concerned about the eternal than the temporal, we face some unique challenges in the financial area. Why? Because so much of what we do with money is obviously temporal. Think about it. That new car quickly becomes obsolete. The freshly painted house soon needs painting again.

The funds you saved for college are all used up. As a matter of fact all the "things" that can be done with money are temporal except for one: giving. If we give money to God's work, we will benefit personally with eternal reward: "Not that I seek the gift, but I seek the fruit that abounds to your account" (Phil. 4:17). In addition, money used to support a missionary or a pastor has an eternal benefit because of the people he or she will impact, who in turn will impact others for eternity.

So, since most of what we do with our money is going to be burned up, what is eternally significant? An often-quoted poem answers that question: We have only one life, and it will soon be past; "only what's done for Christ will last." The soul of man and the Word of God are all that will last. It follows, then, that only things that involve people or God's Word will not be burned up—our families, our neighbors, our prayers and fellowship, our godly character, our giving, and our witnessing, among others. Does this mean we should not be concerned about money and possessions? No, not at all. Money is necessary and useful for buying food, shelter, clothing, and the like while we are here on earth. But money and possessions will be of no benefit when we pass from this life into the next. "Riches do not profit in the day of wrath, / But righteousness delivers from death" (Prov. 11:4).

The choice, then, is between an eternal legacy that lasts or a legacy that does not last. Consider these words of Canadian real estate baron Stephen Sander: "I'd make a $20 million deal and come home and say, 'This is insane. I need something for my soul. I'll leave behind a real legacy not just real estate.' "[2]

A Glimpse of Eternity

Not only does it help in our decision making about money and family to know what is important to God, but it also helps us to understand where we are going and how long we are going to be there.

Christ has gone ahead to prepare a "mansion" for us (see John 14:2), its size to be determined by the degree to which we accomplish God's business. We are going to heaven, which contains a city that is a solid cube —1,500 miles by 1,500 miles by 1,500 miles (see Rev. 21:10–27). This could mean 2,250,000 square miles on each tier of the cube extending 1,500 miles upward —like a huge skyscraper. If each tier was one mile apart, the surface area of the city would be seventeen times larger than the surface of the earth and fifty-eight times larger than the earth's land surface. It is a city made of gold and every precious stone—jasper, sapphire, emerald, chalcedony, sardonyx, sardius, chrysolite, beryl, topaz, chrysoprase, jacinth, and amethyst, not to mention the gates of pearls and transparent glass. As we think about heaven, our pursuit of earthly possessions should pale in comparison; we should have a desire for our families to be there. And that means we should teach our children to understand where they are headed and what is really important.

Think again about the quote at the beginning of this chapter describing a huge rock in the North, where every thousand years "a little bird comes . . . to sharpen its beak. When the rock has thus been worn away, then a single day of eternity will have gone by." Does that grab you as it does me? I have been here forty years, and I can comprehend another forty. But I cannot comprehend eternity. Yet that is where I am going to be soon. If I die before finishing this sentence or if I happen to live another forty or fifty years, either way eternity is coming soon. It is soon for you too. The key is to be ready.

That's why we have to make the right decisions now about our money and our family so we will be positioned for the trip into eternity. As Randy Alcorn, pastor and faculty member at Western Baptist Seminary, said in his book *Money, Possessions, and Eternity,* "Someday this upside down world will be turned right side up, and nothing in all eternity will turn it back again. If we are wise, we will spend our brief lives on earth positioning ourselves for the turn."[3]

"Positioning ourselves for the turn." How do we do that? We do it by constantly focusing on the eternal (people) in the realm of the temporal (materialism). It is obvious that all people are important to God, and consequently all people should be important to us. However, in this book we will focus on a strategic subset of all people—the family.

Many couples have expressed to me the sadness they feel that their children "just didn't turn out right," even though they gave them everything money could buy. Many marriages have experienced significant stress as a result of poor short-term decisions about money. If we do not think long-term and see ourselves as Jim did, standing before God, we will make short-term decisions that could have significant negative consequences in the future. As Ron Blue has said, "The longer range your perspective, the better your decisions today." But why is it so difficult to think long-term in the area of money?

I believe it has to do with the way we think. When my oldest son was three years old and someone would distract him, he didn't know how to say, "You made me lose my train of thought," so he would say, "You got my thinking off!"

For many of us today, our thinking is off because we have subtly bought the lies of the world. Let me give you some illustrations. One of the first things we do to prepare a financial plan for an individual is to look at his or her tax return and ask for a listing of assets and liabilities. When we ask whether there are any debts, it is not uncommon for the person to say, "No, except my home mortgage." My unspoken response is, "What do you call that if it is not debt?" We have become so used to a home mortgage (it's all-American to have one) we do not even call it debt anymore. That thinking has come from the world.

Although the Bible tells us that "the borrower is servant to the lender" (Prov. 22:7), the world tells us we are smart to get a loan. Bank commercials entice us to borrow so we can deduct the interest from our tax returns. After a while we begin to think we must be dumb if we don't go get a loan.

Another illustration of worldly thinking versus biblical thinking is the whole area of retirement. From the time we get out of school we are programmed to think about quitting. Our focus is on that magic time at age fifty-five, sixty, or sixty-five when we can retire. It is so ingrained in us that we work long, hard hours, many times at the exclusion of our families, so that one day we won't have to work at all. Yet the Bible is clear about living a balanced life, working at the same time we are storing up treasures in heaven rather than on earth.

In the next few chapters we will look at the difference between *prosperity*—the accumulation of goods on this earth—and *posterity*—the heritage we leave in the generations that come after us. Then in Part 2 we will look at a new kind of balance sheet: the life-overview balance sheet, a unique definition of capital that includes the social and spiritual legacy, as well as our financial provisions, we will leave our children. We will examine how we earn our money in light of this balance sheet. Finally, in Part 3 we will look at how we can best use our money to leave the proper social, spiritual, and financial legacy to our children.

In this book we will also look at the financial paradox of life: When we are young and need the money and a big house, we do not normally have them, but when the children are grown and gone we can afford the large house and have more money than we have ever had. We will look at the reasons why couples buy a big house just as the children leave and the big house is no longer needed. We will also consider the interesting fact that no one ever gets to the end of his or her life and says, "I wish I'd worked more and spent less time with my children."

As the twentieth century closes and the twenty-first century dawns, we will bid good-bye to the most prosperous century in the history of mankind, when financial wealth has been created and multiplied as never before. Other nations look to America as the model; they want to accomplish what we have accomplished by way of our increased standard of living. But what have we really accomplished?

We have increased our lifestyles, but in the process haven't we also lost our ability to really live? We have amassed wealth, not wisdom. We have given our children toys, not time. We have children who have been taught to consume rather than work; we have fathers who don't know their children, and marriages that do not work or last. We have been in a rush to run a race without understanding the finish line. Could it be that we are being robbed of our very lives because we are not thinking correctly about why we have money and what we are to do with it?

I realize that many of the observations shared in these pages have the potential to offend some readers. That is not my intent. I also recognize that these observations and thoughts are not the last word on the subject. However, as a fellow sojourner who grapples with these tensions, I hope you will be challenged as I was to think about money and your family. May this book be a resource to enable you to live *A Life Well Spent.*

For Further Reflection

1. Why is it so difficult in today's society to think in terms of the eternal?

2. Didn't Jim do a lot of "good" things during his life? Won't those count for something? Consider 1 Corinthians 3:13–15 in your answer.

3. What would you do differently if you knew your actions would really impact your rewards in eternity?

4. What comes to mind when you think of heaven?

5. How does a correct view of heaven affect the way you live today?

2

PROSPERITY

THE ACCUMULATION OF GOODS

Measure wealth not by the things you have, but by the things you have for which you would not take money.

Anonymous

Riches do not profit in the day of wrath,
But righteousness delivers from death.

Proverbs 11:4

I sometimes take my wife, Julie, and our children with me on business trips. One absolutely gorgeous fall day we took an overnight car trip to visit a prospective client. As we neared the address we'd been given, Julie was navigating with the scribbled directions in hand and I was keeping my eyes peeled for signs of the house. We seemed to be getting farther and farther from the town where the new clients said they lived, but we hadn't come to the right address yet.

Then we saw it! What a magnificent place! Set back probably three-quarters of a mile off the road was a house that looked like it had come right out of *Southern Living* magazine. It was resplendent, especially with the leaves glistening in the autumn sun. As we drove down the winding lane with trees on each side we could see what seemed to be dozens of thoroughbred horses grazing in the fertile pasture that surrounded the house and numerous outbuildings. Closer to the house, we could see a tennis court and gazebo off to one side and a pool and cabana in the back near the barn. Julie and I agreed this was a "dream setting."

It seemed obvious that the couple who owned this place must be extremely prosperous and successful, with riches beyond measure. As we were about to find out, however, that observation was false. We were actually more prosperous than they were!

How is that? you ask. It has to do with a correct understanding of prosperity, success, wealth, and riches. My purpose here is to clarify the actual meaning of these words in light of God's Word so we can understand the fullness of their meanings rather than limit them to the narrow context in which they are used today.

In today's society these four words are used interchangeably and in many cases synonymously. For example, we might say, "That person is wealthy" or "That person is successful" and mean the same thing. But *do* both words really mean the same thing?

Defining Prosperity, Success, Wealth, and Riches

To begin, let's look at the definition of these words according to the original *Webster's Dictionary of the English Language*, considered to be the final authority in the field of lexicography.

It is interesting to note that although Webster struggled for most of his first fifty years with the issue of Christianity, he finally realized his need for the saving power of Christ and became a Christian. This is important in that all of his definitions utilize God's written Word as a key to the meanings of the words. He considered education useless without the Bible.[1]

Webster also understood that any age or society could destroy its language by changing the definitions. As a result, he defined basic words that were universal and had meanings that could not be disputed as a result of a sect or cultural change. It is in this context that the following words were defined:

- *Prosperity:* advance or gain in anything good or desirable; successful progress in any business or enterprise; success; attainment of the object desired. *Prosper:* to be successful; to succeed. *Prospering:* advancing in growth, wealth, or any good.
- *Success:* the favorable or prosperous termination of anything attempted; a termination that answers the purpose intended; prosperous, fortunate, happy.
- *Wealth:* prosperity, external happiness; riches; large possessions of money, goods, or land; that abundance of worldly estate that exceeds the estate of the greater part of the community; it is a comparative thing—a man may be wealthy in one place but not so in another.
- *Rich* or *Riches:* wealthy; opulent; possessing a large portion of land, goods, or money, or a larger portion than is common to other men or to men of like rank; an abundance of something; having more in proportion than our neighbors.

These definitions show that prosperity and success can be used synonymously because they both imply action or progress toward a desired end. Wealth and riches, on the other hand, can also be used synonymously because they are both comparative in nature and relate to material possessions and external things.

So do you want to be prosperous and successful or wealthy and rich? Was my prospective client prosperous or wealthy? By looking at these words as they relate to the world we live in we can get a clue to the answer to this question.

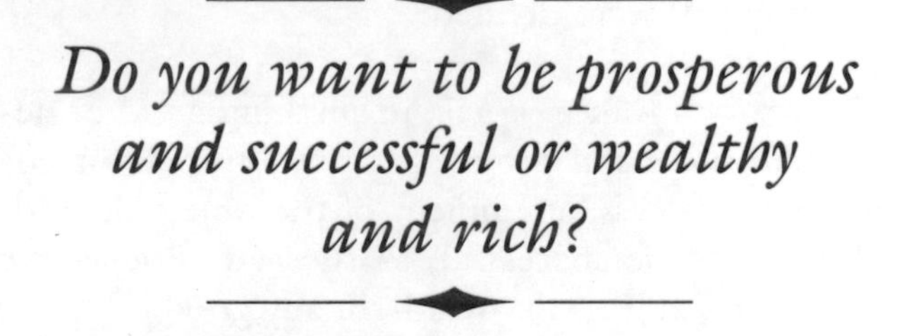

The World's Definition of Prosperity

To understand how the world defines prosperity, we need only reflect on how we evaluate and think about people. Have you ever been waiting for someone and he or she drives up in a very nice, new car? What was your immediate thought? If you are honest, I am sure you'll admit thinking, *This person must be successful.* What about visiting a college friend you haven't seen in quite some time and you find his or her home in a nice subdivision? Don't you think he or she must be doing quite well to live there? Don't you think this person is prospering? (This is what Julie and I thought as we approached the southern-style mansion.) What if the neighborhood you are driving through is not so nice? Do you think, *Hmmmmm, he (or she) isn't doing so well?* What about when you find out that the new member of your church is a doctor? This person is a success, right? Why? Because of what he or she does.

We think this way because the world has influenced us to believe prosperity and success are measured in one of three primary ways: material possessions, position (vocation), and power.

The world readily uses *material possessions* such as cars, boats, houses, and nice clothes to measure prosperity or success. When we see such things we make comments such as, "He has a successful company" or "She is successful" without any knowledge of the person's real financial condition or of how these things may have been obtained.

As I have learned in my business, such observations can be very misleading. I have met with many individuals who drove expensive foreign cars and wore custom-made suits—and had more debts than assets. Their prosperous and successful appearance was actually a mirage.

If we use material possessions to measure prosperity or success, what about the drug dealer or the crime kingpin? What about the young couple who receives a large inheritance? Are they successful? The world measures success more by perception than by reality. This means that for many people image is everything; accumulating things to look prosperous is the ultimate motivation in everything they do.

The second way the world measures prosperity or success is a person's *position*, or vocation. Consider how you feel about a doctor, a lawyer, or an accountant versus a cook, a janitor, a missionary, or a schoolteacher. If you are honest you would probably admit that you have not used the words *janitor*, *secretary*, or *missionary* and *success* in the same sentence recently. In the world, positions that generate the most income or require greater knowledge and education are the ones deemed successful, and vice versa. We tend to elevate knowledge —without regard for wisdom. This is shown by how easily impressed we are by an individual's degrees from certain universities.

The third way to measure prosperity is *power*. We consider persons successful if they hold an office of power or authority. Consider the judge or the senator or the chief executive officer of a large corporation. In each of these positions the individual has the authority to make decisions and the power to carry them out. On the other hand, we do not consider the rank-and-file employees successful because they have very little control over their own destiny. Someone else is making the decisions for them.

In God's economy a person is prosperous and successful as a result of the process he or she goes through in working, regardless of the fruit of that work.

Five years ago when my first book, *Money and Your Marriage*, was published, I experienced firsthand the subtlety of the world's thinking on prosperity and success. After calling on a client in another town I decided to visit the local Christian bookstore to see if they had my book and to see how many copies they had sold. Much to my surprise (as well as my chagrin), they had never even heard of my book! On the way home I happened to drive by another Christian bookstore in another small town. Being a glutton for punishment, I decided to stop and see how many they had sold. Here again, they had never even heard of it.

Why did I stop at those stores? Because I knew that in book publishing, success is measured by the number of copies sold. If I was to be considered a success as an author, my book needed to sell a lot of copies. But is that true success?

It is obvious that the world has linked wealth and riches inextricably to success and prosperity. But how does God define these words?

God's Definition of Prosperity

Wealth, *riches*, and *prosperity* are not new terms. They are used many times throughout Scripture. For example, in Ecclesiastes 2:4–10 we read Solomon's words:

> I made my works great, I built myself houses, and planted myself vineyards. I made myself gardens and orchards, and I planted all kinds of fruit trees in them. I made myself waterpools from which to water the growing trees of the grove. . . . I had greater possessions of herds and flocks than all who were in Jerusalem before me. I also gathered for myself silver and gold and the special treasures of kings and of the provinces. . . . So I became great and excelled more than all who were before me in Jerusalem. . . . I did not withhold my heart from any pleasure, for my

> heart rejoiced in all my labor; and this was my reward from all my labor.

Solomon had it made. He was wealthy beyond measure. He had possessions, position, and power. "The weight of gold that came to Solomon yearly was six hundred and sixty-six talents of gold. . . . So King Solomon surpassed all the kings of the earth in riches" (1 Kings 10:14, 23). Let's take a closer look at Solomon's comments to gain insight into the difference between the world's definition of prosperity and God's definition. We will begin by examining the different meanings of possessions, power, and position.

The Process, Not the Possessions. Bill, a friend of mine, has very few possessions and lives quite modestly with his wife and four children in a small house on the other side of town. I met Bill about three years ago at the urging of an acquaintance. He had just trusted Christ and begun to grow as a believer. Shortly after we met, Bill called to tell me he had lost his job. Since that time he has had several jobs, most of which pay slightly more than minimum wage.

Though Bill is a talented, personable fellow, he just has not been able to get a job that pays well. But through it all, I have never heard him complain. He loves his wife and children and works hard to make sure there is food on the table. I cannot help but think of the mansion in heaven Bill will live in.

In God's economy a person is prosperous and successful as a result of the process he goes through in working, regardless of the fruit of that work. In other words, if you do your work heartily and with the right attitude, you are a success regardless of your income level or what possessions you accumulate. Look at what Solomon said:

> Then I hated all my labor. . . . Yet he will rule over all my labor in which I toiled. . . . Therefore I turned my heart and despaired of all the labor in which I had toiled under the sun. . . .
>
> There is nothing better for a man than that he should eat and drink, and that his soul should enjoy good in his labor. This also, I saw, was from the hand of God. For who can eat, or who can have enjoyment more than I? (Eccles. 2:18–20, 24–25)

Solomon realized the possessions his labor had produced actually amounted to nothing. The vineyards, silver, gold, flocks, and herds did not fulfill him. Though he may have appeared successful, he realized he was not. He knew if God did not give him the ability to enjoy the process of his labor, it was all vanity.

> He who loves silver will not be satisfied with silver; nor he who loves abundance, with increase. . . . The sleep of a laboring man is sweet, whether he eats little or much; but the abundance of the rich will not permit him to sleep. . . .
>
> Here is what I have seen: It is good and fitting for one to eat and drink, and to enjoy the good of all his labor in which he toils under the sun all the days of his life which God gives him; for it is his heritage. As for every man to whom God has given riches and wealth, and given him power to eat of it, to receive his heritage and rejoice in his labor—this is the gift of God. . . .

> There is an evil which I have seen under the sun, and it is common among men: a man to whom God has given riches and wealth and honor, so that he lacks nothing for himself of all he desires; yet God does not give him power to eat of it, but a foreigner consumes it. This is vanity, and it is an evil affliction. (Eccles. 5:10, 12, 18–19; 6:1–2)

Thus we see that the *process* of working is the real blessing. Success is found in the process, not in the product. As Henry Ford observed, "Work is the only pleasure. It is only work that keeps me alive and makes life worth living. I was happier when doing a mechanic's job."[2]

This means riches and wealth (material possessions in greater quantity than others around you) may be a curse or a blessing, depending on whether you have been empowered by God to enjoy them. Matthew Henry, in his *Commentary on the Whole Bible*, said:

> Riches are a blessing or a curse to a man according as he has or has not a heart to make good use of them. God makes them a reward to a good man, if with them he gives him wisdom, and knowledge, and joy, to enjoy them cheerfully himself and to communicate them charitably to others. He makes them a punishment to a bad man if he denies him a heart to take the comfort of them, for they do nothing but tantalize him and tyrannize over him.[3]

Isn't it interesting that money, the very thing the world says makes people prosperous and successful, may actually be a curse? Does this mean money is evil and we should not have it?

No, money is not evil, and yes, a rich man can be successful. The key is God's empowerment. I believe the way God empowers us to enjoy the fruit of our labor is by giving us the proper perspective about it. This perspective means we hold with open hands any material possessions that have come from Him. And remember: *Everything* we have comes from Him! "What do you have that you did not receive?" (1 Cor. 4:7). We enjoy our possessions, but we don't let them own us; we express an attitude of "relaxed nonchalance" toward them, managing them enough to be good stewards but not allowing them to consume us.

Too often, however, we do allow riches to consume us. It has been said that 95 percent of those who have been tested with *persecution* pass the test, but 95 percent of those who have been tested with *prosperity* fail. Perhaps this is why, in this prosperous country, we have one of the world's highest divorce rates, drug abuse in epidemic proportion, corruption in government, and increasing crime throughout the land.

The first difference then, between God's definition of prosperity and the world's definition is that godly persons who are prosperous have the ability to enjoy the labor God has given them to do and they hold the fruit of that labor with open hands. You are prosperous in a small house and an old car if you have God's perspective. Likewise, you are prosperous if you live in a large house and drive a new car as long as you hold them with an open hand. If your attitude toward your possessions is not empowered by God it does not matter what you earn or where you live. In an article in *Moody Monthly*, Dennis Haack wrote, "Abraham and Sarah were wealthy and they pleased God. Jeremiah was desperately poor, but no failure."[4] The trappings that money can buy have nothing to do with prosperity.

Character, Not Power. The second difference between God's definition and the world's definition of prosperity is His view of *power*. Instead of seeing power and authority as signs of prosperity and success, God sees *character* as the true indicator.

There is no greater place of power in all the world than the office of the president of the United States. In the last election, I found it interesting, however, that many of the American people were influenced by the place of power to the point of overlooking the character of the man who would occupy that office. It is incredible that the power of a presidential candidate can cause people to overlook his character—even if he might be immoral or ungodly.

The trappings money can buy have nothing to do with prosperity.

God says character is what is important, not power. "The LORD does not see as man sees; for man looks at the outward appearance, but the LORD looks at the heart" (1 Sam. 16:7). If a person has power but is prideful, dishonest, disloyal, arrogant, driven, and greedy, he or she is not successful in God's eyes.

If a person is full of pride, any success that person may have in the world is invalidated by God. "God resists the proud, but gives grace to the humble" (1 Pet.

5:5). The reason is that the attitude of pride is, "I have this power because of my ability," while the attitude of humility is, "God has given me this ability." Success results from character qualities such as integrity, honesty, teachability, loyalty, responsibility, courage, determination, endurance, hospitality, generosity, and humility.

We gain a clearer understanding of this definition by looking at the character quality of humility. The world says you are successful if you hold a place of power—CEO, corporate executive, or president of the company. God says if you want to be first, you should be last. If you want to be exalted on the day you move into eternity, you must exhibit humility now.

> But when you are invited, go and sit down in the lowest place, so that when he who invited you comes he may say to you, "Friend, go up higher." Then you will have glory in the presence of those who sit at the table with you. For whoever exalts himself will be abased, and he who humbles himself will be exalted. (Luke 14:10–11)
>
> Therefore humble yourselves under the mighty hand of God, that He may exalt you in due time. (1 Pet. 5:6)

This is not false humility that says, "I am no good," but humility that acknowledges total dependence upon a sovereign and almighty God. When we understand God's definition of prosperity we recognize that any honor or power that comes in this life is simply a gift from Him; He gets the credit. You can be a success to God while you're the president of the company or the number-one salesperson as long as you realize that what you are is a gift from Him.

Just as we could not measure success by possessions, neither can we measure success by power. The prophet Daniel is a good illustration of a person who was successful because of his character, not his power. Daniel was one of only a few Jewish youths whose character was such that they were put in the king's personal service. Daniel was elevated to a place of prominence, not because of his power (the king had the power), but because he was discerning, knowledgeable, humble, and thankful (see Daniel 1–6). In other words, Daniel was successful because of his character. Power can be fleeting, but character has staying power. As Albert Einstein once commented, "Try not to become a man of success but rather try to become a man of value."[5]

Obedience, Not Position. The final difference between God's definition and the world's definition of prosperity is God's view of *position*. Instead of seeing position as a symbol of prosperity and success, God sees obedience as the true indicator.

Quite a while ago, I consulted with a young man who had followed his father and grandfather into business. He had a nice income, a nice house, nice cars, and all the extras. However, as I got to know him, I soon learned things were not as they appeared. The young man was actually miserable. He had been seeking counseling for quite some time, and his marriage was in trouble. As we worked through the situation, it was clear that he had not been obedient to God in choosing a vocation. He had followed in his father's and grandfather's footsteps because that was the easiest path and he could make more money than if he started a new business, as he felt God wanted him to. Once he left the family business and started his own business, his life gradually came back into focus. He had less money, but he was content.

The world deemed this young man a success when he worked in the family business. Why? Because of the riches and material possessions he was able to accumulate as a result of his income. But was that the work God wanted him to do? Would this man be able to say to God what Jesus was able to say: "I have glorified You on the earth. I have finished the work which You have given Me to do" (John 17:4)?

We are all called to different vocations. We cannot all be doctors, developers, accountants, or lawyers. We also need cooks, letter carriers, police officers, grocers, plumbers, printers, and truck drivers. Therefore, regardless of a person's vocation, only God really knows if he or she is successful. We do not know the degree of someone else's obedience. We can measure his or her wealth and riches, but not his or her success; we are only successful if we are obedient.

Is an excellent teacher who makes thirty thousand dollars less successful than a professional athlete who sits on the bench and makes three hundred thousand dollars? In God's definition, their obedience and the degree to which they have maximized the abilities He has given them are the keys to their success. Their income has nothing to do with it. They both could be failures if they are not doing their best or if they disobeyed God in choosing their vocation. Since it is God who gives us the ability to make wealth (see Deut. 8:16–18) and God who designs each of us to perform different functions, then the income we earn cannot possibly be the measurement of success. Dennis Haack summarized this idea in his article, "Which Success Really Counts?":

> Wealth or poverty, fame or obscurity, power or helplessness, fulfillment or boredom—these are not

> the essence of life nor of spirituality. They are not the marks of success or failure. God calls us to faithfulness, to live a life of moment-by-moment trust and obedience in whatever circumstances He has ordained for us. We find true success only by faithfully knowing and doing the Word of God.[6]

The Successful Completion of Right Things

These issues of success and prosperity come together in the book of Joshua. One verse, in particular, contains God's definition of success:

> This Book of the Law shall not depart from your mouth, but you shall meditate in it day and night, that you may observe to do according to all that is written in it. For then you will make your way prosperous, and then you will have good success. (Josh. 1:8)

As I wrote in *Money and Your Marriage*, "I am successful as I am in the process of being obedient and carefully doing all that God's Word says to do. For example, I am successful as I train and love my children (Eph. 6:4; Deut. 6:6–8) and love my wife (Eph. 5:28). These verses do not guarantee or promise financial blessings if I do what God's Word says. Rather, they free me up to realize that I can be successful whether or not I have money. Money is not the barometer! A successful person may or may not have money. Likewise, a person with money may or may not be a 'success'."

Do you remember the lesson I learned with my other book? The challenge for me was to realize that I was a success and prosperous because I had been obedient to do what God had called me to do (write the book). It did not matter how many copies I had sold.

Isn't that what Webster said? He defined success as "the favorable or prosperous termination of anything attempted." In Joshua 1:8, the things that are to be attempted come from God's Word. As we do these things we are successful. Does this mean that non-Christians cannot be successful? No, they have attempted and completed many endeavors. The problem is if the endeavor, even though it is successfully completed, is not important to God; then it will be for naught on Judgment Day. Obviously, then, success in God's economy is not just the successful completion of anything attempted but rather successful completion of *the right things!*

If we demoralize the definitions of success and prosperity and define them as products (cars, houses, boats, vacations, and so on) rather than as the process (obedience, character, etc.), we will make temporal decisions instead of eternal ones.

What are the things we should do, whether in word or deed, that bring glory to God? As I've reflected on the Word and counseled hundreds of couples, I've discovered three key areas related to money and family that are the right things in God's eyes.

The first is described in Colossians 3:23: "Whatever you do, do it heartily, as to the Lord and not to men." You are successful as you work hard at what God has called you to do, regardless of what your income is. Second, "Let nothing be done through selfish ambition or conceit, but in lowliness of mind let each esteem others better than himself" (Phil. 2:3). You are successful as you have harmony in your marriage and love your spouse and manage healthy relationships with others regardless of whether you have a place of power. Finally, "His saints . . . are preserved forever, / But the descendants of the wicked shall be cut off. / The righteous shall inherit the land, / And dwell in it forever" (Ps. 37:28–29). You are successful as you train and love your children, regardless of your position.

"The real issue is redefining success, rethinking the basis of pleasure and fulfillment and practicing a life that builds that."[7] If we demoralize the definitions of success and prosperity and define them as products (cars, houses, boats, vacations, and so on) rather than as the process (obedience, character, etc.), we will make temporal decisions instead of eternal ones. We will tend to sacrifice our families on the altar of material possessions. We will sacrifice relationships including our marriages in pursuit of position. We will sacrifice our character in the quest for power. We must rekindle the true definitions penned by Webster and confirmed in Scripture in order to be truly prosperous and successful. We must pursue the correct definition of prosperity rather than the false, shallow definition implied in wealth and riches.

We exhibit the correct understanding of prosperity, success, wealth, and riches when we use these words in a context that expresses the things God says are key: "He is a successful father." "They have a prosperous family because their children have such good manners." "You're a successful wife and mother." And conversely, if we see a Mercedes go by, we should think, *He has riches. I wonder if he is prosperous.*

What Julie and I did not know as we drove toward that beautiful home I described at the beginning of this chapter was that the couple who lived there had riches, but they were not prosperous in the areas that mattered. It was a third marriage for both, and they had incredible challenges with their children, several sets of stepchildren, and their former spouses. The litany went on and on. They would have gladly traded their gorgeous "spread" for something God says is much more important, their *posterity*. In the next chapter we will look more closely at the heritage we leave to coming generations.

For Further Reflection

1. Think about ways you use the words *success, prosperity, wealth,* and *riches*. In what context do you usually use them?

2. In what ways might your new understanding of the definitions of *success, prosperity, wealth,* and *riches* affect your day-to-day life?

3. What can you do to help your children understand the fullness of the true definitions rather than the narrow definition that is so prevalent today in the world?

4. Do you realize now that you are more successful than you might have thought before reading this chapter?

3

POSTERITY

THE HERITAGE WE LEAVE TO COMING GENERATIONS

Children are the living messages we send to a time we will not see.

J. W. Whitehead

A family is the caretaker of the soul of man.

The Estate Sale video,
White Lion Pictograph Productions

The future is purchased by the present.

Samuel Johnson

Behold, children are a heritage from the LORD,
The fruit of the womb is His reward.
Like arrows in the hand of a warrior,
So are the children of one's youth.
Happy is the man who has his quiver
full of them.

Psalm 127:3–5

As I walked off the jetliner one Sunday afternoon in early June, I quickly scanned the airport sign for an indication of where I should go to meet my clients. They were flying their private, four-seater plane to take me to their home 150 miles away. I quickened my pace as I spotted arrows pointing to the terminal for private and commuter aircraft. I was sure they would be waiting for me, and sure enough, as I walked across the tarmac to the plane, Jim Montague and his dad, Paul, came forward to greet me.

Paul, now in his early seventies, had started a small manufacturing business several years ago and was still active in the business along with Jim, who was in his forties. They were clients of mine, and over the years we had become good friends while maintaining a strong client/adviser relationship.

When they realized the entire Montague family was going to be together for an upcoming family reunion, Jim and Paul decided it would be beneficial if I would come and share with their entire family the financial principles I had helped them implement in the business. As the small single-engine plane swooped low over the cornfields and the barn next to their home to land on the grass-covered runway, I had no idea what I was about to observe.

At least one hundred people representing four generations were at this family reunion. As I mingled through the happy throng, meeting many of the family members, I noticed a unity and harmony that is rare in many families today. I was especially impressed with the relationships between the generations. The children and adults interacted in a very mature and respectful manner, seeming to genuinely enjoy each other. The jet skis on the small lake next to the house were in constant use, with the older kids and adults helping the younger kids. The food spread on tables under the shade trees provided a setting for wide-ranging conversation as the family members ate together. But what, I wondered, was behind the interactions I was observing? Why did this family get along so well? I decided to ask Paul, the patriarch of the group. After all, I was just beginning my own family and I welcomed his advice.

Paul explained to me that in six generations of Montagues there had been eleven ministers, four lay ministers, fifteen music ministers, twenty Sunday school teachers, seven missionaries, seven professors, seventeen school teachers, and twelve Christian college students. *What a heritage!* I thought. What was the secret to ensuring that generation after generation would pass on to the next the essentials for leading lives that counted for eternity?

When I asked Paul this question he motioned for me to follow him into the house, where he pulled an old book from a shelf in his library and dusted off its cover. He flipped a few pages and stopped, then handed it to me and said, "Russ, this is the key to what you see out here today." On the page were words spoken by his grandfather, Daniel Montague, more than a hundred years ago, on August 2, 1882. At the age of seventy-seven he had addressed a similar family reunion, telling his loved ones,

> Now if you wish those principles established and carried out by your descendants, inculcate into the minds and hearts of your children the principles of religious instruction. Everything, almost, that is evil, everything, almost, to subvert the religion of Jesus Christ, is at work; and it is absolutely necessary to train the rising generation in the principles of Christ. It is the great work of the country. For Christian institutions, friends, we have reason this day to thank God; and what I ask of you who are now on the

stage of action is that you should be true to the principles of Christ and humanity, to the name and characteristics of the Montagues that have gone before you.

There was the key: the rising generations. *The children!* What I observed at this family reunion was a family's godly posterity. Their unity and harmony was the result of a focused plan to pass on Christ's principles from one generation to the next. And the only way these principles could have gotten from Daniel Montague in 1882 to the young children playing before me that Sunday afternoon was for succeeding generations to do their part while they were on their "stage of action."

As I left the family gathering the next day I was struck with the irony that, although I had gone to the Montagues to share financial principles and talk with them about money, they had shared with me a principle that was much more important, *the principle of posterity.* As I have thought about that day, I have realized that I, like most people I know, did not seem to be very interested in posterity. I spent more time being concerned about my finances than my posterity. Why?

I believe the reason financial wealth has replaced posterity in our thinking is twofold. First, as we discussed in the last chapter, we do not know the true definition of prosperity. We have falsely defined prosperity as money, and we have pursued that goal rather than true prosperity —a godly posterity.

Second, we do not know what posterity means, either! In this chapter I will share what I've learned about the real definition of posterity. It is my hope that you will come to realize, as I did, that money is simply a tool to invest in our posterity.

Posterity Defined

Posterity is defined in Webster's dictionary as "descendants; children, children's children . . . indefinitely; the race that proceeds from a progenitor." Posterity, then, is our descendants—our children and grandchildren.

At this point you could conclude that this book has nothing for you if you are single or childless. To the contrary! If you think of posterity as any others you may influence for eternity, then these principles apply to you just as easily as they apply to a married couple with children or grandchildren. When you see the term *children* think of the individuals you are discipling or influencing, and remember that God is concerned about people —all people. Therefore, if you impact people through discipleship and a godly influence, you have a posterity in the family of God and the principles discussed here apply to you.

We all leave some kind of influence and mark on the next generation.

Understanding that *posterity* really is the only mark I can leave on the generations that come after me has changed the way I look at money and possessions. Many people start their business careers with the objective of creating a name for themselves and leaving a mark on society by making a lot of money and becoming a recognized figure in the community. Many persons even hope to have their name on a building or two as a lasting tribute to their contribution to society. But before you set those kinds of goals for yourself, let me share some verses that put this thinking into perspective:

> Their inner thought is that their houses will continue
> forever,
> And their dwelling places to all generations;
> They call their lands after their own names.
> Nevertheless man, though in honor, does not
> remain;
> He is like the beasts that perish. . . .
> Do not be afraid when one becomes rich.
> When the glory of his house is increased;
> For when he dies he shall carry nothing away;
> His glory shall not descend after him.
> Though while he lives he blesses himself
> (For men will praise you when you do well for
> yourself),
> He shall go to the generation of his fathers; . . .
> Man who is in honor, yet does not understand,
> Is like the beasts that perish.
>
> *(Ps. 49:11–12, 16–20)*

> But the day of the Lord will come as a thief in the night, in which the heavens will pass away with a great noise, and the elements will melt with fervent heat; both the earth and the works that are in it will be burned up. (2 Pet. 3:10)

These words make it clear that it is impossible for us to leave a lasting mark through material means. The only mark that will truly last is our posterity. This concept is vividly illustrated by the first-century disciples. The mark these men left is not in material things but in the fact that Christianity is still alive and well some two thousand years after they lived.

The Bible on Posterity

As I have studied this concept I have been amazed at how many times the Bible uses words, such as *descendants*, that are related to posterity. The following list contains just a few of these verses; I hope they will help you get a feel for the significance the Bible puts on pursuing posterity instead of financial wealth. Here are some of those scriptural insights:[1]

Who is the man that fears the LORD?
Him shall He teach in the way He chooses.
He himself shall dwell in prosperity,
And his *descendants* shall inherit the earth.
(Ps. 25:12–13, emphasis added)

I have been young, and now am old;
Yet I have not seen the righteous forsaken,
Nor his *descendants* begging bread.
(Ps. 37:25, emphasis added)

For the LORD loves justice,
And does not forsake His saints;
They are preserved forever,
But the *descendants* of the wicked shall be cut off.
The righteous shall inherit the land,
And dwell in it forever.
(Ps. 37:28–29, emphasis added)

Mark the blameless man, and behold the upright;
For the man of peace will have a *posterity.*
But transgressors will be altogether destroyed;
The *posterity* of the wicked will be cut off.
(Ps. 37:37–38 NASB, emphasis added)

Let his *posterity* be cut off,
And in the generation following let their name be blotted out.

> Let the iniquity of his fathers be remembered before
> the LORD,
> And let not the sin of his mother be blotted out.
> Let them be continually before the LORD,
> That He may cut off the *memory* of them from
> the earth.
>
> *(Ps. 109:13–15, emphasis added)*

> Tell your children about it, let your children tell their children, and their children *another generation.*
>
> *(Joel 1:3, emphasis added)*

> The *memory* of the righteous is blessed,
> But the name of the wicked will rot.
>
> *(Prov. 10:7, emphasis added)*

Many principles can be drawn from these verses, but two primary ones stand out. First, every person will have a posterity. We all leave some kind of influence and mark on the next generation. The question is, What type of posterity will you leave? The second primary principle is that a righteous, godly posterity will last forever, but a wicked posterity will not be remembered.

You may be mentally arguing that a wicked posterity *can* last from generation to generation. "One generation of thieves leads to another," you may be saying—and that is true. But in the end, *when eternity comes*, the righteous will inherit the earth and the wicked will be remembered no more.

The legacy of our posterity (whether it be righteous or wicked) is determined to a large degree by the decisions we make today while we are on the "stage of action." The awesome thing about it is we do not get a second chance to be on stage. As we go through life we must choose whether to pursue money and the things money can buy—or a godly posterity. These are not mutually exclusive, and the balance of the two will be developed throughout this book; but in all too many cases posterity is sacrificed on the altar of the world's definition of prosperity, which is financial wealth and riches.

The legacy of our posterity . . . is determined to a large degree by the decisions we make today while we are on the "stage of action."

Anyone can leave a mark on the next generation regardless of his or her income, position, or possessions. How? By inculcating into the minds of his or her children the "principles of Christ," as Daniel Montague said. To do this, we must know what these principles are; they must come from the Bible. If we don't use the Bible as our standard, we will, by default, teach our children the ways of the world. The world's way of thinking could result in roleless marriages for our children. They could be taught to think that money is the key to happiness, encouraged to pursue jobs only for the money they will earn, and led to see no problem in allowing others to raise their posterity while they pursue positions and power.

The Big Picture

In these first three chapters we have seen that we are truly prosperous and successful only as we leave a godly posterity. We have clearly seen from Scripture that money and material possessions will not last but that our posterity will. We have also seen that the type of posterity we leave is determined by the decisions we make during our lives, and in life we only get one shot from one generation to the next.

In Part 2 we will look at how we can get a higher return on life and still handle our money wisely.

For Further Reflection

1. Are your words consistent with your actions? If not, what changes do you need to make in your life to be consistent?

2. Write something you would like to say to a reunion of your posterity one hundred years from now.

3. What steps do you need to take to maximize your effectiveness during your remaining years?

Part Two

How to Get a Higher Return on Life

4

The Life-Overview Balance Sheet

Distribution of Our Financial, Social, and Spiritual Capital

Maybe a lesser return on your investments makes sense in exchange for a higher return on your life.

Dick Davis Digest

Then I hated all my labor in which I had toiled under the sun, because I must leave it to the man who will come after me.

Solomon in Ecclesiastes 2:18

Julie and I are the proud parents of three sons—Clark, 10; Reed, 8; and Chad, 5. And, we have faced the challenge of determining how much time I should spend working, how quickly I should amass money for retirement, if at all, and so on. We have also discussed what our involvement in the church should be, especially now when we have young children, and how—and if—our involvement should change as they mature. On top of all this, we struggle with modeling a work ethic for the children while still finding time to spend with them while they are young and most impressionable.

It is fine to understand the correct definitions of wealth, prosperity, success, and riches, and it is great to desire a godly posterity. But how does this all work out in everyday life? How do we get a higher return on life and still handle our money wisely?

The diagram of what I call the life-overview balance sheet (fig. 4.1) depicts the integration of the two concepts we have been developing—money and family or financial prosperity and posterity.

Understanding the Balance Sheet

The line at the top of the diagram represents our lives. We have each been given a certain amount of time, short or long, to be here on planet earth. We must maximize the time we have, living consistently with what God says is important. Two of my favorite verses speak to this need to live purposefully:

> Look carefully then how you walk! Live purposefully and worthily and accurately, not as the unwise and witless, but as wise—sensible, intelligent people; making the very most of the time—buying up each opportunity—because the days are evil. (Eph. 5:15–16 AMP)

> And this I pray, that your love may abound yet more and more and extend to its fullest development in knowledge and all keen insight—that is, that your love may display itself in greater depth of acquaintance and more comprehensive discernment; so that you may surely learn to sense what is vital, and approve and prize what is excellent and of real value—recognizing the highest and the best, and distinguishing the moral differences. (Phil. 1:9–10 AMP)

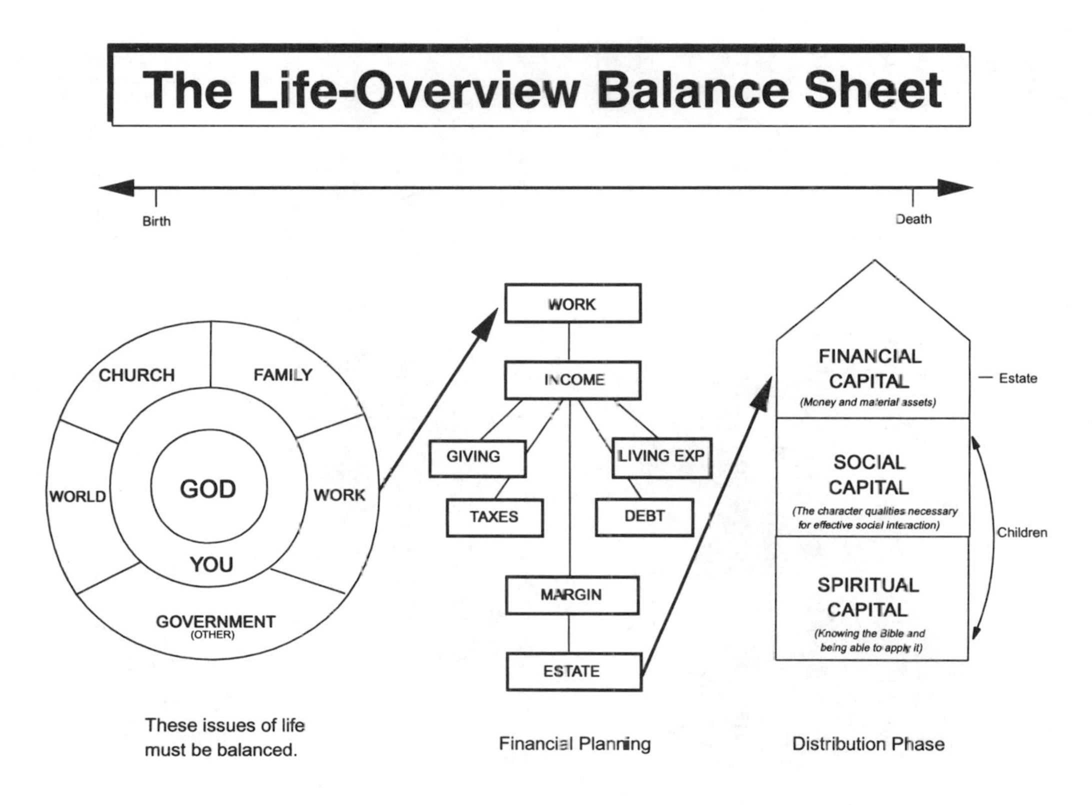

The Life-Overview Balance Sheet
Birth
Death
CHURCH
FAMILY
WORLD
GOD
WORK
YOU
GOVERNMENT
(OTHER)
These issues of life
must be balanced.
WORK
INCOME
GIVING
LIVING EXP
TAXES
DEBT
MARGIN
ESTATE
Financial Planning
FINANCIAL
CAPITAL
(Money and material assets)
— Estate
SOCIAL
CAPITAL
(The character qualities necessary
for effective social interaction)
Children
SPIRITUAL
CAPITAL
(Knowing the Bible and
being able to apply it)
Distribution Phase

FIGURE 4.1

As we live our lives, the challenge is to be involved in the areas God says are important (things shown in the wheel on the left side of the diagram). We know from Scripture that church attendance is important; we are not to forsake our assembling together (see Heb. 10:24–25). We know we are to be salt and light in the world (Matt. 5:13–16) and at the same time we're to work hard (Col. 3:23) to provide for our families (1 Tim. 5:8) and spend time with them (Deut. 6:6–8). We know that posterity is of utmost importance to God and that material possessions, though they may be part of our lives, are not vital to God and not of eternal value.

All the spiritual and social training that goes on in our posterity is behind the scenes. It cannot be measured on a balance sheet and observed like our financial capital.

It is my observation, however, that in spite of this knowledge, most people (Christians included) are working hard and fast and long in the pursuit of a prosperity defined by money and possessions (including things listed in the middle part of the diagram), only to realize toward the end of their lives, when they plan the distribution of their money and possessions (the financial capital shown on the right side of the diagram), that they didn't adequately train their posterity, their children, to handle that capital.

The house on the right side of the diagram represents our children and the three forms of capital—spiritual, social, and financial—that we will leave to them. If you have no children, you leave these three components to the people you have discipled during your life. Let's take a closer look at these types of capital.

Spiritual capital, or spiritual resources, includes an understanding of biblical absolutes, of how to come to Christ, of God's character, of how to walk by faith and to trust God, as well as biblical principles of money management, childrearing, marital relationships, and so on. Spiritual capital is knowing the Bible and being able to apply it. It is using the absolute truths of God's Word to determine right from wrong, good from evil.

Social capital is a resource base that allows one to relate to society. All the character qualities necessary for effective and productive interaction in society are part of a person's social capital. For example, responsibility is a necessary trait to hold a steady job, as are punctuality, honesty, integrity, loyalty, discipline, and the like. Morality is a critical component of social capital and includes ethics, conformity to rules of right conduct, and distinguishing right from wrong.

Moral capital, or morality, flows out of spiritual capital—an understanding of the absolute values of God's Word—and is lived out in the realm of social capital. Consider the illustration of sex within the context of marriage. We learn from God's Word (Heb. 13:4) that sex is only appropriate in marriage. We live out such absolute truths by how we conduct ourselves in the social capital area, in this case relating to the opposite sex in a chaste manner, abstaining from sex until married.

Financial capital is money and material assets such as land, stock, and jewelry. If we do not balance all aspects of life early in our vocations, we will have missed some critical time to invest in the spiritual and social capital of our posterity. Furthermore, the financial capital one has amassed will be for naught if the other forms of capital are not present.

When we need the time, money, and the big house for the children, we don't have it to give them, and when we finally get the time, money, and the big house, we don't need them; the children have started families of their own.

The best way to illustrate the integration of money and family is to think of the house in the diagram as a literal house. The foundation of the house represents spiritual and social capital, and the house itself represents the financial capital. Who would build a house without a foundation? That would be foolish. Yet many people are busy building financial houses (working to make more money) and neglecting the houses' foundations (their families).

Note that the foundation of most real houses cannot be seen. Similarly, the spiritual and social training that goes on in our posterity is behind the scenes. It cannot be measured on a balance sheet and observed as can financial capital. Remember what 2 Corinthians 4:18 says: "We do not look at the things which are seen, but at the things which are not seen. For the things which are seen are temporary, but the things which are not seen are eternal."

Let me make one final observation about the foundation: It cannot be constructed by an absentee builder. Jesus trained His disciples by being with them: "He appointed twelve, that they might *be with Him* and that He might send them out to preach" (Mark 3:14, emphasis added). To train our children we must spend time with them. Spiritual and social capital cannot be built into our children except as we spend time with them—and this doesn't mean just quality time but quantities of time.

Unfortunately, many parents do not recognize the impact of a lack of time with their children until much later in life, when they're planning their estate and specifying the distribution of their financial capital. At this point the financial capital itself becomes a nonissue; all energies are directed to the building of the foundation, hoping to instill responsibility and godly instruction on how the estate is to be used. However, just as older concrete and boards are less pliable and moldable, so are children when they are older and more set in their ways. That's why it is essential (although admittedly difficult) to balance the issues on the life-overview balance sheet throughout your family's life together; this way you continually build spiritual and social capital to leave to your posterity as well as financial capital.

The Challenge

The challenge is to balance the need to earn a living with the goal of training and impacting your posterity. The difficulty of this challenge is due to our posterity's most urgent need for us at the exact time our income needs are greatest and the time pressures from our work are the most demanding. As many experts have said, the most strategic time in the lives of our children is their first ten years, when the majority of the training and instruction in values takes place. This also happens to be the very time most fathers begin their careers and have the greatest time pressures at work. Too often the career pressures win the tug-of-war. "Curiously, American families currently devote greater hours to paid work during the state in life when they are most apt to have childrearing responsibilities and fewer hours (if any at all) during the twilight years of life (between ages 55 and 70) when they are least apt to have dependent care duties."[1]

It all seems backward, doesn't it? When we need the time, money, and the big house for the children, we don't have it to give them, and when we finally get the time, money, and the big house, we don't need them; the children have started families of their own.

We take two risks if we do not accept the challenge of balancing these aspects of our lives. The first is that we could get to the end of our lives and have financial capital but no relationship with our posterity. The life of J. Paul Getty, the well-known millionaire who died in 1976, illustrates the consequences of this risk.

- The rich oil king once said that he would have sacrificed his entire fortune in exchange for a successful marriage. He . . . made five attempts at marriage.

- His millions . . . bought him neither peace nor tranquility of mind. He once said that there are a lot of things that money cannot buy. It could not buy health, nor affection, nor good digestion, nor a long life. He also said that money could be an obstacle to happiness.
- Several of his wives said they could not share the life of a man devoured by a passion for business.
- Some of his children [were] against him. His grandson was [kidnapped].[2]

The second risk we take if we don't balance our lives is that our children will be ill prepared to handle what we have worked to accumulate for them if we do not train them in how to handle it. As a result, we could feel as Solomon did, that it all is vanity (see Eccles. 2:18–21).

Several months ago I met a gentleman whose lament echoed Solomon's. As we visited it was obvious that he had been quite successful at amassing financial capital but very unsuccessful at building spiritual and social capital into his children. As a matter of fact, he and his children barely spoke to each other. Their relationship had been strained for quite some time. He wanted to leave them his financial assets, but they really did not want to have anything to do with him or his possessions.

He admitted that he had never been around while his children were young, and he acknowledged that some of the current friction was probably a result of this. His business schedule had him leaving home on Monday and returning on Friday. When he was at home the perfectionist expectations he placed on his children alienated them from him. I wish this scenario were a rare exception, but my observation is that it is all too common.

A tremendous amount of financial capital resides in the hands of the post-World War II generation (some reports put this figure at six to eight trillion dollars). The assets of these parents are ready to be passed to the baby-boomer generation and their children, but most are ill prepared to handle it. They were not trained in how to handle it because their parents were too busy earning that money. To compound the problem, the baby boomers have been so busy chasing the same false definition of prosperity as their parents (that is, money and possessions) that they have not trained their children in how to use those assets, either.

Right now you face three challenges, regardless of whether you are just beginning your family and career, or you are middle-aged, or you are like the elderly gentleman who was trying to sort out his estate for children who had no interest in it:

- The challenge to **balance life** while earning your money. (We'll discuss this in more detail in Chapter 6.)
- The challenge to use money wisely and make good financial decisions in order to **free up time** to invest in your posterity (to be discussed in Chapter 7).
- The challenge to **strategically invest** the time you've freed up (to be discussed in Chapters 8–13).

As you study these chapters I hope the words of Socrates ring in your head, as they do in mine: "What mean you fellow citizens, that you turn every stone to scrape wealth together and take so little care of your children to whom you must one day relinquish it all?"

For Further Reflection

1. What are some of the challenges you face in balancing work and family?

2. Why do you think God allows the existence of the time tension we face in the early years of our families? Why don't we have the money earlier in life when we need it rather than later in life when we don't need it?

3. In what ways are you scraping wealth together, as Socrates said, to the exclusion of your children to whom you must one day relinquish that wealth?

5

The Principle of Time Replacement

How to Add Posterity Time to Our Schedules

Did you ever see a tombstone with a dollar sign on it? Neither did I. I have known hundreds of men who lived as though their only ambition was to accumulate it, but I have never known one who wanted a final judgement of himself to be based on what he got. A man wants people to read in his obituary, not a balance sheet of his wealth but a story of his service to humanity.

Homilope

The days of our lives are seventy years;
And if by reason of strength they are eighty years,
Yet their boast is only labor and sorrow;
For it is soon cut off, and we fly away.
So teach us to number our days,
That we may gain a heart of wisdom.

Psalm 90:10, 12

At a recent conference we held for our clients, Dr. James Dobson, a noted authority on the family, was one of the speakers. During his talk he made an interesting comment: "If a couple loses their kids, they have nothing." He went on to say that the greatest threat to the family, and subsequently the greatest contributor to losing our posterity, is having no time.

I agree wholeheartedly with his assessment, and I am convinced that one of the major reasons for parents' lack of time is bad financial decision making. In Chapters 6 and 7 we will look at how financial decision making affects time. But before we do that, in this chapter we will look at time itself, the critical component to leaving a godly posterity.

What Is Time?

In his book *Living on the Ragged Edge*, Chuck Swindoll defined time as "a stretch of duration in which things happen."[1] Our lifetime is the "stretch of duration" we have to make things happen. The challenge is to make things happen in the area of posterity versus the area of money and materialism.

The other principle about time is that, for richer or for poorer, we all have the same amount of it. We all have twenty-four hours in each day that we can spend as we choose. Once it's gone, each increment of time is irretrievable; it cannot be repeated or relived. This is why strategic use of our time is so critical. We want to do the right things with it, the eternal things, the purposeful things. Leon Danco, an internationally recognized authority on the management of family-owned businesses, made this statement in his book *Beyond Survival*:

> A working lifetime is less than 500 months. Every time we take off one of those monthly watchband calendars and throw it away, we are throwing away an increasing percent of what is left. That realization is sobering. Time is not recallable. No warranties, no inventory, no quality assurance, no return of the deposit. Time just runs out. . . . Time is our most finite and irreplaceable resource.[2]

BUYING TIME

We all have the same amount of time each day to allocate among the various issues of life—work, family, church, and the world. We also have the same opportunity to "buy time" for investment in our posterity.

Let me illustrate. An amount of something (in this case it's time) that is not committed to a specific purpose is called ***margin***. So when we refer to the concept of "buying time" we are talking about building margin. In most homes today families have used their money to buy appliances such as microwaves, dishwashers, washing machines, and clothes dryers that free the mothers from domestic chores so they have more time to direct toward other pursuits. And what about dads? Money has bought riding lawn mowers, automatic sprinkler systems, and so on to likewise free them from domestic chores.

The key is how Mom and Dad use the "free time" these conveniences create. Is it directed toward the social and spiritual capital of their posterity, or toward some other pursuit? Too often instead of using this time for training our children and modeling godly priorities for other people, we have used it in the pursuit of more money. As a result the typical person's work time has expanded from forty-one to forty-seven hours per week.[3] Instead, it is critical that we use the margin we've created to focus on what God says is important—our posterity.

There is a fine line between indulging our children and using our money to invest in memories and create closeness.

Just last year Julie and I chose to use some extra money to redo the basement to provide a greater play area for the children. We also decided to cement a portion of the yard and put up a basketball court so the boys and I had a place to play ball, something I hope will help me stay emotionally close to them as they grow. We have also used some extra money to do things with the boys on weekends: attending football games, going ice skating, playing miniature golf, and so on. Although some people might call these items living expenses, I see them as investments in my posterity.

When our three children were all under six years old, we allocated some money for a housecleaning service to buy Julie some time to invest in the kids. For a couple of years this was a good investment of money; it freed her to do the things she needed to do with the children. However, we are no longer investing money that way now that the children are in school.

Dads may find that they need to invest in a lawn service rather than spend all weekend working in the yard to the exclusion of their young children. Of course, once the children are old enough to work with Dad or even do some of the work and begin to learn a work ethic, a lawn service may not be a good investment. The key is to use our money wisely to buy time—not things—unless, of course, the things enhance the time (as microwaves and dishwashers do, for example). We need to be creative and resourceful in our thinking in this area, taking into account our station in life and the ages of our children.

There is a fine line between indulging our children and using our money to invest in memories and create closeness. The point to consider is that money is a tool, and when it is used to create time that can be spent training our children, that is potentially a much better investment than putting the money in the bank or the stock market so we can retire sooner. I am not suggesting that you should not look ahead and store up financial resources for the future to some degree. But I encourage you to realize that money is utilitarian, and in addition to stocks, bonds, and real estate, some of it can and should be invested in the higher priority of rearing a godly posterity. The amount and manner in which this is done should be a matter of prayerful consideration between husband and wife.

As a side note, it is important to realize that it costs more today to buy time than it did when the family was not so fragmented. In past decades, a young couple's extended family provided free help with such things as baby-sitting and the loan of tools (Grandpa's nearby shop was stocked, so Dad didn't need to buy them). Today, it is still possible to buy time without money, i.e., by swapping baby-sitting and sharing tools with trusted friends and neighbors, but it is much more difficult than it used to be. This is one reason we need to manage our money wisely—so we have available resources to "buy" the time we need for our families.

Obstacles That Steal Time

Just as we can use our money to buy time to invest in posterity, we can also be blocked by four major obstacles that steal the time we have with our posterity. These four obstacles are our inability to say no, our inability to slow down, our inability to turn off the television, and our inability to control our desire for possessions. Let's take a closer look at each of these obstacles.

Our Inability to Say No

Dennis Rainey, the director of the Family Ministry of Campus Crusade for Christ, has said that the word *no* "may be the most powerful word in the English vocabulary." Powerful, I would agree, because it has the greatest potential to affect the balance in our lives.

It is impossible to live balanced lives and focus on the best if we don't say no to a lot of "good" things. Having the ability to say no means we have thought through what is eternally important and we have set goals for our family, church, work, and the world. These goals are unique to each individual; they form the grid through which all decisions are made. Parents need to use the following nine words frequently to buy time: "No, that is not on our list of priorities!"

As Richard A. Swenson said in his book *Margin*, "To be able to say no without guilt is to be freed from one of the biggest monsters in our overburdened lives. If we decline, not out of self-serving laziness but for God-honoring balance and health, this level of control will not only protect our emotional margin (and time) but will actually increase it."[4]

It is important to realize that it costs more today to buy time than it did when the family was not so fragmented.

I remember when our first child was born. A friend of ours commented that we were going to be "out of pocket" for the next six years. It did not take us long to understand what she meant, especially when our other children came along. During that stage in our lives, when our children were babies and toddlers, they demanded so much of our physical time we had to say no to a lot of good things—such as teaching Sunday school—that we had enjoyed in the past.

Julie and I have concluded that if we are to keep some time in our schedules to strategically build spiritual and social capital into our children (something we call posterity time) we will practice the **principle of replacement**. Figure 5.1 illustrates this concept. It means we will attempt to only add new projects or commitments to our schedule if they will replace something else in our schedule. This presupposes that we have a schedule that is balanced and not overscheduled to begin with at our current station in life.

FIGURE 5.1

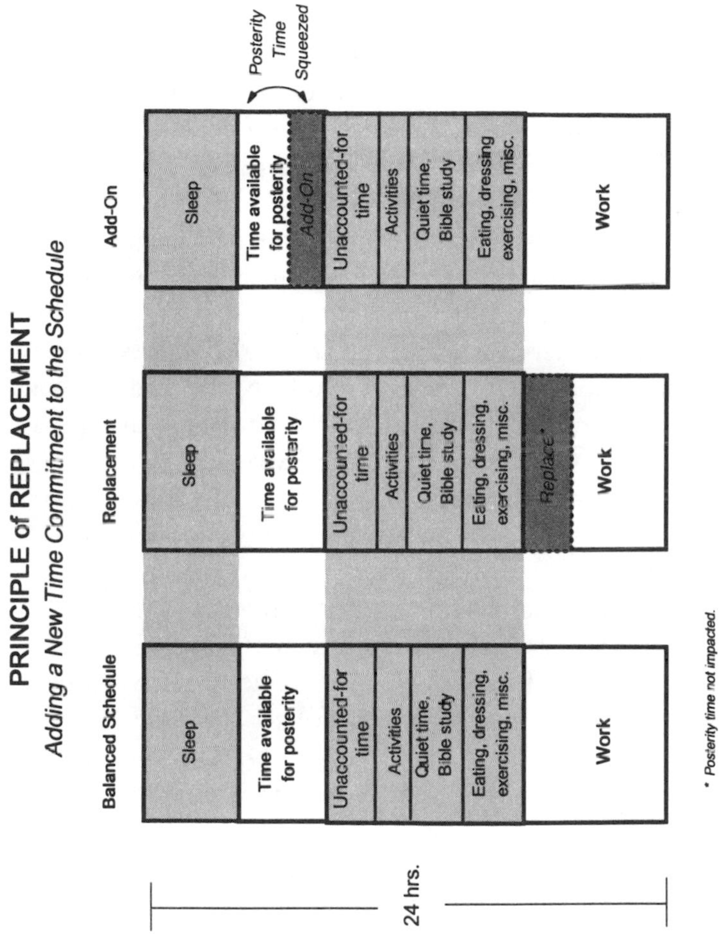

PRINCIPLE of REPLACEMENT

Adding a New Time Commitment to the Schedule

24 hrs.

Balanced Schedule	Replacement	Add-On
Sleep	Sleep	Sleep
Time available for posterity	Time available for posterity	Time available for posterity
		Add-On
Unaccounted-for time	Unaccounted-for time	Unaccounted-for time
Activities	Activities	Activities
Quiet time, Bible study	Quiet time, Bible study	Quiet time, Bible study
Eating, dressing, exercising, misc.	Eating, dressing, exercising, misc.	Eating, dressing exercising, misc.
	*Replace**	
Work	Work	Work

Posterity Time Squeezed

** Posterity time not impacted.*

Note that in the chart a balanced schedule includes time for Bible study and activities (such as kids' soccer and school programs), plus time for sleeping, dressing, eating, exercising, and work, as well as unaccounted-for time and time available for posterity. Although I may share some activities, including Bible study, with my children, it seems I still need to leave some unplanned posterity time in my schedule.

I can sleep less, forego exercise, or neglect my spiritual time to create posterity time; but in the long run if I get my posterity time from these time slots, I will be too tired to share with my children—and besides that, I will have nothing to share. Therefore, the addition of new time commitments to my schedule are usually a trade-off between work and posterity time.

An obvious argument at this point is, "But I must work as much as I can because I need the money." *Aha!* Therein lies the key. We need to make good financial decisions and handle our money prudently so we have the option to replace work time with posterity time. Managing our finances is critical, not to have more money or to be able to retire, but to buy time for our posterity.

Understanding this principle made it easy for me to say no when our church asked me to be an elder four years ago. Because of the time demands of our young children and my work at the time, it did not fit into my schedule. It could only be an add-on. In other words, to say yes to that commitment would have reduced the time margin I had built into my schedule, and that margin was my posterity time. However, if I am able to reduce some of my work time in the future, I could choose to replace that work time by serving on the board of elders and still have time in my schedule for the children.

Unfortunately, too many of us do not say no; we simply add more and more onto our schedules. What ends up getting replaced is any time we would have had for our posterity. My encouragement to you is to build a schedule that leaves a margin of time for your posterity. Only say yes if it replaces something else that's already in your schedule.

The second obstacle that takes away from our time is our inability to slow down.

Our Inability to Slow Down

In today's world everything goes fast, and we strive constantly to see if we can make it go faster. If the computer makes us wait five seconds for data, we want a new computer. If the fast-food line takes more than two minutes, we get impatient and visit a different fast-food place the next time. *Progress* is the term we use to describe this increased speed and the ability to utilize every second to the maximum, but many times I wonder if it really is.

Richard Swenson offered some intriguing comments in *Margin*. He wrote:

> Progress has given us unprecedented affluence, education, technology and entertainment. We have comforts and conveniences other eras could only dream about. Yet somehow, we are not flourishing under the gifts of modernity as one would expect. We have ten times more material abundance than our ancestors yet we are not ten times more contented or fulfilled. Margin has been stolen away and progress was the thief. We must have room to breathe. We need freedom to think and permission to heal. Our

> relationships are being starved to death by velocity. No one has time to listen, let alone love. Our children lay wounded on the ground, run over by our high-speed good intentions.[5]

It seems to me that this frenetic pace is a real detriment to our ability to establish the building blocks of our posterity. Why? Because it leaves us no leisure time. Consider this statement by Gil Schwartz in a *Fortune* magazine article: "Before capitalism, the pace of work was relaxed. Our ancestors may not have been rich, but they had an abundance of leisure. When capitalism raised incomes it also took away the time."[6]

The addition of new time commitments to my schedule are usually a trade-off between work and posterity time.

Similarly, Jeremy Rifkin, in his book *Time Wars*, commented, "According to a Harris Survey, the amount of leisure time enjoyed by the average American has decreased 37 percent since 1973. Progress was billed as leisure-permitting and time-gifting. The opposite has been true." He continued by stating, "The modern world of streamlined transportation, instantaneous communication, and time-saving technologies was supposed to free us from the dictates of the clock and provide us with increased leisure. Instead there seems never to be enough time. Tangential or discretionary time, once a mainstay, an amenity of life, is now a luxury."[7]

James Dobson once watched people as he sat in an airport and later noted his observations in the December 1992 issue of the *Focus on the Family* newsletter:

> I saw busy, exhausted men and women who appeared to be hours behind schedule. Would it really create an international crisis if they pulled up a chair beside me and watched the world go by for a few minutes? I know! I know! Planes don't wait!
>
> What a price we pay for the speed at which we run! Already, the new year we greeted last January has dwindled to its twilight hours. It will soon recede into history. Most of us remember these last 12 months as a blur of activity. There was so much work to do. There were so many demands on our time. There was so much pressure.
>
> Meanwhile, what should have mattered most was often put on hold—or shortchanged—or ignored altogether. Millions of children received very little love and guidance this year from their busy parents. Husbands and wives passed like ships in the night. And our spiritual nature languished amidst overcrowded schedules and endless commitments. There must be a better way to approach the responsibilities of living . . . the enduring virtues of family, friendship and our Christian faith. Over-committed schedules and exhausting lifestyles undermine them all. That *could not* be God's will for us! . . .
>
> As we approach the new year, will you join me in making a renewed effort to slow the pace of living?[8]

Our age's unique inability to slow down its pace was vividly illustrated to me when Julie and I joined another couple on a visit to the Biltmore House in Asheville, North Carolina. This house was built by the Vanderbilts of railroad-industry fame and fortune in the mid-1800s. What caught my attention as we went on a tour was the large eating rooms with adjoining sitting areas. Much emphasis was placed on mealtime in those days, and it was not uncommon for each meal to last two hours. So much of the space in the house was allocated to the dining rooms and breakfast areas because the family spent a lot of time there in conversation and dialogue—before, during, and after the meal. It was during these conversations that values and training of the next generation took place.

What a contrast to the typical American family today—ours included! Just the other night I rushed home from work in time to eat a quick bite with the family (a hurried, fifteen-minute meal) before Julie had to rush to a meeting and I had to take the oldest boy to soccer practice. It is not unusual to have this scenario replayed by many families night after night and weekend after weekend. We probably don't spend two hours a week together as a family around meals, let alone two hours at each meal!

Dr. Patrick Malone commented:

> We have created a society in which we're living too close, too fast and with too much stress. . . . It's largely a result of the decline of the traditional family, in which children lived in a home with two parents, the family ate meals together at regularly scheduled times and fathers interacted with their offspring. . . . Families don't sit down at the dinner table together anymore. A lot of families don't even

have a regular dinner time because they might not all be there at the same time.[9]

As our society has become more urban and less agrarian our pace has quickened and the demands on our time have increased. Fifty to one hundred years ago, children spent much time with their parents in their workplace whether in the shop or on the farm or in the kitchen, an arrangement that was useful for training and instruction. This is much less true today. Children typically don't have the opportunity to go with Dad to his place of work. This means time is needed during other parts of the day for the training and instilling of values that fifty years ago happened in the course of the family's daily togetherness. Is it any wonder time replacement is needed?

Build a schedule that leaves you a margin of time for your posterity. Only say yes if it replaces something else that's already in your schedule.

Society's hectic pace is accelerated by kids, newspapers, magazines, junk mail, debt, commutes, community interests, geographic logistics, and so on because they demand more of our time. The changes in geographic logistics illustrate this nicely. In the smaller communities of fifty years ago, churches, schools, Bible studies, work,

Little League games, and the like did not require the time commitment to commute that they do today in urban America. You could walk to the ball field and school, usually in five or ten minutes. Although this situation exists today in smaller communities across America, it has become the exception rather than the norm as more and more people commute longer and longer distances to their jobs. Time is stolen by these long commutes, our pace is accelerated, and the quality of our lives suffers. Dr. Swenson summed it up when he wrote, "Chronic overloading also has a negative effect on our spiritual lives. We have less time for prayer and meditation, less energy for service and less interest in relationship."[10] To that I might add: including our posterity!

To redeem teaching time and cultivate relationships, Julie and I have been very careful to guard our evenings and especially our family's mealtimes. We do this by minimizing the number of things we say yes to, including meetings or groups that meet in the evenings during the week. We are convinced that a relaxed mealtime together and the time after the meal are great opportunities to pass on values. We do not answer the phone during the meal. We use that time for conversation about the day's events, for reminding our boys about good table manners, and for helping them learn how to relate to and talk with adults. The after-meal time is a good time to wrestle and play games together. It is also a time when Julie and I can read stories to the boys. If the weather permits we may also work in the yard or do projects around the house together. Overall, we try very hard only to do things that include the children while they are young. This is why I do not play golf; it is something they cannot enjoy yet. But I hope to start playing golf again when the boys can join me on the course.

I also recognize that many good activities—Bible study and soccer for instance—can occur during the week. I know it is next to impossible to avoid a few nights where the meal is eaten in a rush before we fly out the door to some activity. Still, we may be able to cut out a Bible study or an activity so we can spend more time with our children.

As a working dad who needs to travel for his job, I have also tried to make sure if I do have to travel over a weekend I make up for it at a later time by taking a day off. I try not to be gone on weekends at all, but it sometimes happens. I also try not to be gone too many nights in a row.

The process of deliberately slowing the pace is unique to each family. The key is to be aware of the problem and take positive steps to change. Otherwise a hectic pace is a killer of purposeful and strategic living; it shortchanges our posterity.

A third obstacle that steals time is the television.

Our Inability to Turn Off the TV

It has been said that children watch as much as five to seven hours of television per day and spend no more than three minutes per day talking with their fathers. Is it any wonder why it is difficult to impart correct values to our children with this kind of disparity? Julie and I have found if we really focus on the priority of raising a godly posterity there is very little time for television. I have found the following essay to be quite insightful as well as revealing:

The Twenty-Third Channel

The TV set is my shepherd, my spiritual growth shall want. It maketh me to sit down and do nothing

> for His name's sake, because it requireth all my spare time. It keepeth me from doing my duty as a Christian, because it presenteth so many good shows that I must see.
>
> It restoreth my knowledge of the things of the world, and keepeth me from the study of God's Word. It leadeth me in the paths of failing to attend the evening worship services, and doing nothing in the kingdom of God.
>
> Yea, though I live to be a hundred, I shall keep on viewing my TV as long as it will work, for it is my closest companion. Its sounds and its picture, they comfort me. It presenteth entertainment before me, and keepeth me from doing important things with my family. It fills my head with ideas which differ from those set forth in the Word of God. Surely, no good thing will come of my life, because my TV offereth me no good time to do the will of God; thus I will dwell in spiritual poverty all the days of my life.[11]

I do not suggest that you throw out your television, although some have done this. (If you do remove the television, make sure you replace your TV time with activities that contribute to your child's social and spiritual development.) My recommendation is that you take the lead in training your children and passing on values. Do not let the television do it. Sometimes when you watch television together with your children you can use the television program as a teaching tool.

A fourth obstacle is our desire for more and more possessions.

Our Inability to Control Our Desire for Possessions

In many cases, the toys and gadgets we purchase consume our time instead of giving us more leisure time. "Paradoxical as it may seem, modern industrial society, in spite of an incredible proliferation of laborsaving devices, has not given people more time to devote to their all-important spiritual tasks; it has made it exceedingly difficult for anyone, except the most determined, to find any time whatever for these tasks," observed E. F. Schumacher. "In fact, I think . . . the amount of genuine leisure available in a society is generally in inverse proportion to the amount of laborsaving machinery it employs."[12]

We have more and more stuff to take care of, clean, repair, and look after. For example, we may buy a second home or even a third home and feel it is a good investment for our posterity, but if we end up spending more time looking after the home than we spend enjoying it with our posterity, it could be a detriment. It may be okay to have a boat as a means of creating family memories, but if your time is consumed with taking care of the boat and you don't spend time with your children as a result of it, the boat becomes a negative factor for your posterity. Or if the boat puts you under financial bondage so you have no flexibility to do anything but work to pay it off, it may be a negative.

The time we have to lay the foundation of social and spiritual capital goes so fast that if we are not careful we will miss it. When children are young, they *want* to be around us and they will allow us to train them, but as they get older this changes. As they reach the teenage years the teachable moments decline.

Jeff Davidson wrote what I would consider a classic article for the *Focus on the Family Magazine* in June 1986. It captures the essence of this issue:

> At quarter of eight, as always, he is sitting across the breakfast table of his 17 winters, sipping and munching, palming back a sheaf of morning hair, an ear cocked for the mating call of the school-bus horn.
>
> And I miss him.
>
> Yet there he sits, still within my reach, intent on blading over each open space of toast with strawberry jam. He misses me not; his sapling mind is rooted in the unsentimental present. He is revving up for flight.
>
> Seven minutes to go before the end of breakfast, a hundred breakfasts to the end of childhood. This swiftly coming September, his place will be empty and unsticky, and he will be licking from his fingers the strawberry jam of independence. Like the generations before him, from the feet of Socrates to the backfield of Notre Dame, he will be a college man.
>
> Wait a minute. Please. Who says there's such a big hurry to launch his frail bark on the river of whatever? Where have all the breakfasts gone? The bedtime stories, the birthday cakes, the finger paints, the knee patches, the model planes, the goalie gloves and hiking boots, the facts of life, the SATs, the hanging gardens of disco?
>
> We have awakened together 6,000 times. Can't I save any of them for a sunless day? We have eaten 15,000 meals together; why can I remember only half a dozen? What has been the rush?
>
> I crystal-clearly remember the bubbly babble and the rhythmic creaking of the crib; and, after they

lanced his infant finger, bearing the white bundle of him shrieking through the street, his mother pale at this first communion with pain. I know we wrestled on the big country bed, and I am sure I heaved his wiry, giggling frame over and over and over onto a green mountain of hay—I remember the smell of fresh-cut grass and his hair shimmering in the mottled sunlight. But then I skip all the way to some black-night downpour in the Maine woods: he is laughing against the rain and spinning the front wheel of his bike so I can squint at a sodden map in the dim, spotted glow of its headlight. The next thing I know, we are posing triumphant on the peak of an Alp.

But what about the valleys? Where are the Tuesdays, the Februaries? When was 11 years old? Whatever happened to 1978? Did we let the rest of it speed away in homework assignments, the purchase of sneakers and vacant Sunday afternoons? Why didn't we take more trips to the moon?

We talked about chocolate ripple and subordinate clauses and the four-minute mile—but did we ever get around to love, honor, truth?

He does not hear me thrashing through these last-minute woods: he stirs his placid coffee and blithely leans the spoon face-down against the saucer.

And yet, if I could look into the present and stare it to a standstill, I would freeze his spoon in mid-coffee and hold this semiprecious moment sharp and clear forever. The breeze leafs gracefully through the open book. Something smells of cinnamon. His mother's arm is raised in an offer of bread, and a faucet drips. I try to keep this ordinary, heartbreaking Now from drifting cloudlike into Later. No one will move a muscle. None of this will ever come again.

A whole fugue of noises will be erased from the sound track of our house. Duet for muffled telephone conversation and slamming door. Concerto for hair dryer, open refrigerator and pre-dawn house key. What is the sound of no guitar strumming?

With the change of season, the markers that show he passed along this trail will fade: the scattered books, open to the last idea that lost his darting interest; the music stand at the crossroads of the living room; the randomly slung seven-layer cake of the week's assorted garments.

No more midnight parleys in that two-man's land between our bedrooms. Requests to determine how was school today will have to be put in writing. We will use the telephone for love and hurt and urgency, where once it was just for matters of lunch and dinner.

For him to see us, from autumn on, will require a decision, an act of the will—not just a friendly jostle in the common corridor of our lives. I wonder how much of me he will afford in his future.

This May Monday, I am still a little more equal than he, but already he patiently explains to me disk drives and computer terminals. How long until I am just a memory chip, programmed for Friday-night dinners?

He glances coolly at his watch, as if all it told was heartless time.

I put a warm reassuring arm around his shoulder. This is not our first rite of passage. We have been flight trainees together since that first nursery-school September, when he was dropped by stroller behind enemy lines. After all, we weathered summer camp and survived the first shave. This too may pass.

God knows I am happy for him. So crack the champagne and let him glide out to sea. Give him liberty or give him life. No matter what, I will never confess that I am a tiny bit jealous of all that youth and romance—that I hope now and again the brittle world will make him yearn for the pliable pleasures of home-cooked tenderness.

Go with lump-throated blessing. Take up your stick and red bandanna and pocket calculator, and to thine own self be true. There will always be a fatted calf in the freezer.

But don't let this night be different from all other nights. Please borrow my razor and hang up no clothes. Sing loud, sweet stereo. Strew the neat spaces of our middle age with vibrant disorder.

We will mark off this countdown with little banners of trivial joy. Under the unseeing nose is where they were hidden the whole time. Don't you see, says the last clue, Monday morning is the treasure. Breakfast is a trip to the moon!

So let us savor this day our daily toast. Rejoice in the peal of knives on jam jars. Tell me, before it's too late, what you dreamed about last night or what you want to be when the world grows up.

The wind sits in the shoulder of his sail, and they are waiting for him. A rush-brush of teeth, a grab bag of books, and the door slams me into silence. I shuffle back to the still-life breakfast table. The foghorn of the school bus wails him to distant shores.

Bye. Thanks for the childhood. See you tonight.

Left at the corner, then straight ahead until you hit the world.[13]

Yes, it's only a short time until our children will only see us at their initiative, so we must redeem the time now, before it is too late. In the next chapter we will analyze our present vocation in light of the needs of our posterity.

For Further Reflection

1. What are some ways you could invest your money to buy more time for your posterity?

2. What obstacles do you face that steal time from you?

3. In what ways do you struggle with the consequences of a hectic pace?

4. What specific steps could you take to reduce the pace in your life?

5. Do you agree that a hectic pace is a killer of purposeful and strategic living? Why or why not?

6. Is it realistic in the 1990s to be able to control your pace?

6

A New Understanding of Work

Analyzing Our Vocations in Light of Our Posterity

They lived in a hurry. He gave them everything a father could provide. She was all a mother could be. But the children grew fast and far away and one day all that was left was fifty years of memories for sale in THE ESTATE SALE.

The Estate Sale video,
White Lion Pictograph Productions

But Martha was distracted with much serving. . . . And Jesus answered and said to her, "Martha, Martha, you are worried and troubled about many things. But one thing is needed, *and Mary has chosen that good part, which will not be taken away from her."*

Luke 10:40–42, emphasis added

When I walked into the house late from work one Thursday night, I could tell by the look on Julie's face she was not happy. My mind raced back through my schedule the past two weeks. I knew I had missed dinner the past three nights due to some projects at work, but I could not see how that would cause her frustration. I had told her I was going to have some late days during the current week, so she should have been expecting it. But as my eyes caught hers, she quickly began to explain how I always seemed to be at work, how it appeared that I was never home for dinner, and the children were, as she said, "growing up without me."

I was incredulous, but as we sat down on the couch and began to talk, the reason for her frustration became clear.

Over the past two weeks I had been gone at night, not only for work-related projects, but also for two functions at the church and for two men's basketball games. In addition to that, Julie and I had hosted a school-board committee meeting in our home one night and had a young couple over on another night to help them with their finances. Fewer than half of the past fourteen nights had been spent with our children. Since work was the culprit the last three nights, it caught the brunt of the blame. The issue, however, was not just work.

Balance is defined as "the ability to keep in equilibrium, to estimate the relative importance or value of something." Julie and I have found that it takes a constant effort to balance our lives and keep the pendulum from swinging wildly past center.

Look again at the circle on the life-overview balance sheet in Chapter 4, which indicates the need to balance the components of family, work, church, world, government, and a relationship with God. It is easy to get out of balance in any of the areas by taking time away from one of the other areas. For example, we could spend so much time involved in the church that we neglect our vocational work. Or we could spend so much time evangelizing the world that we neglect our families. Obviously, being out of balance in any area could make it extremely difficult to meet the challenge of balancing posterity and finances.

Though imbalance can occur in any of the areas mentioned, I am convinced that in modern society the greatest threat to a balanced life occurs because of the tension between family and work. In this chapter we will look at why this tension exists, primarily from the work angle, and offer some suggestions about how to deal with it.

Family and Work

The tension between family and work is great because they both require a great time commitment. Yet the Bible is very clear about our responsibility in each of these areas. For example, Deuteronomy 6:6–8 states that I am to teach my children as I sit in my house, as I walk by the way, and as I lie down and rise up. Sitting, walking, lying down, and rising up require a lot of time! In Proverbs 22:6, I am told to "Train up a child in the way he should go." And 1 Peter 3:7–9 tells me that husbands and wives are to live together in a harmonious and understanding way.

The Bible is also clear about our responsibility to provide for our families. The apostle Paul said if we do not provide for our families, we are "worse than an unbeliever" (1 Tim. 5:8), and if we do not work we should not eat (2 Thess. 3:10).

The issues related to our church, world, and government also require time, and they cannot be neglected in the raising of a godly posterity, as we will discuss later. However, these components are less of a time drain than the two primary areas we are discussing—family and work.

Though imbalance can occur in any of the areas mentioned, I am convinced that in modern society the greatest threat to a balanced life occurs because of the tension between family and work.

Over the years, I have kept excerpts of articles that clearly point out this tension. Here is a sampling that shows the sense of loss when the components of work and family are out of balance:

Billy Graham, evangelist: "The greatest mistake was taking too many speaking engagements and not spending enough time with my family."[1]

Jane Fonda, actress: "The few things I regret in my life are . . . not having put enough time into mothering, wiving, taking care of the inner life."[2]

Pete Petit, CEO of Healthdyne: "I've always tried to convince myself that I've spent quality time with my kids rather than quantity time. Now that I'm 50, I realize I've probably been naive about that. You have to realize that parenting is an art, not a science. All your children are different, and have different needs. I'm sure my children have missed some things because I've spent so much time here at work."[3]

Peter Lynch, author and former investment-fund manager: "My problem is, I operate in only two gears, overdrive and neutral, and it's all been overdrive since about 1982. . . . I had to return from it [family ski trip] early and missed seeing my daughter in a race. I was in here at the office when the market was closed and the family was skiing and I said 'what am I doing?' . . . I haven't been there for Beth, my 7-year-old, either."[4]

Garth Brooks, country music star (commenting on his daughter): "She's already taught me the greatest lesson in life—that *nothing* is more important than family. . . . I see that little girl and think, . . . 'You've been chasing stuff that means nothing, and you've been running away from *this*. . . . The one gift that I want to give this kid is the best gift that my dad and mom ever gave me—attention—to know that every time I looked up from that bench at any sporting event, no matter how far away it was, no matter if I was playing or not, they were there. I don't want to end up coming off a concert tour and hear my daughter say 'Hey, I recognize you from your record albums. You're what's-his-name.' "[5]

Dan Stamp, president of Priority Management Systems: "People often say, 'For now, I'll focus exclusively on my career, but in the future, I'll do more with my family.' But by the time the future comes, by the time the person is ready to be a real parent, he may find that it's too late. The kids are grown up—never to be 5 or 10 years old again. Once those years are missed, there's no going back."[6]

Brandon Tartikoff, former chairman of Paramount Pictures: "Personally, I have learned the hard way that it is one grand illusion if you start believing you can be totally dedicated to the demands of your job without shortchanging your pressing responsibilities to your family."[7]

So how do we balance these two components, work and family? The experience I've gained at Ronald Blue and Company tells me that the key is to have a correct understanding of work and income in order to earn my money correctly. This principle is the focus of this chapter. Second, I need a plan for my family so I know what I am trying to accomplish with them. We will look at the importance of this plan in the chapters to follow.

I am aware that some readers are further along in life and may have already discovered what the celebrities quoted above discovered—that you should have balanced your life a little more. If this is the case, let me remind you that it is never too late. Even if your children are grown and have children of their own you can still spend time with them. You can try to help them avoid making the same mistakes you may have made, and you can encourage them with their posterity.

Variable-Time Versus Fixed-Time Vocations

I am convinced that we should earn our money by working hard and doing our best at the vocation God has equipped us to do during our allotted time here on earth—while at the same time allowing appropriate amounts of time to be with our families. When you are newly married without children, you have more time available to work vocationally because you have responsibility only for your spouse. If you have young children their needs as well as the needs of your spouse are more acute, and the amount of time available for work is squeezed. As the children grow up and move out of the home, your available time to work is once again expanded.

I remember when I began to work at Ronald Blue and Company. Many times I would go to the office on Saturdays to study for the exams to earn my Certified Financial Planner credentials. I took Julie with me, and she helped quiz me for my tests. She encouraged me to practice the ten-key calculator so I could be more adept at doing financial plans. I also used to take two-week business trips to the West Coast to see clients, sometimes taking Julie along so she could visit with her parents while I worked. As the children have come along, however, I no longer have some of those luxuries. My allotted time has been reduced.

Your allotted time to work vocationally will be a function of whether your vocation is what I call a variable-time job or a fixed-time job. In a variable-time job you do not punch a time clock; these vocations are typically not the eight-to-five kind of job but rather work that has fluctuating hours. I work in such a vocation. I am not required to punch in and out each day, but I have certain performance standards that must be met. Some days may be twelve hours long; others are much shorter. Through it all, however, there is always more to do than can be done in a reasonable day, so the pressure to spend more time at the job always exists. That is the character of a variable-time job: The salesman could always make one more sale, the doctor could always see one more patient, and the business owner could also help one more customer. More could *always* be done! The question is, where do you stop?

On the other hand, the fixed-time job is the eight-to-five kind of work that neither requires or expects much involvement beyond the time spent in the office or shop. The factory worker, secretary, nurse, and grocery clerk are examples of those having fixed-time vocations.

At our firm we work primarily with individuals who fall into the variable-time professions—business owners, entrepreneurs, doctors, dentists—since the variable professions typically generate the most income. On the surface it seems that variable-time workers have it made. They have time *and* money for vacations.

On the surface what appears to be a positive of the variable-time job—the higher income—is in many cases a detriment to spending time with family and training up a godly posterity.

These individuals have a challenge, however, that fixed-time workers do not have. They have to constantly guard against overworking. In *Money and Your Marriage*, I defined overworking as any situation where a person is spending hours on his or her vocation to the exclusion of other priority areas, such as family, church, and personal time. The fixed-income worker who is punching a clock does not typically have the pressure to overwork. Most days, he or she puts in eight hours and goes home. However, on the surface what appears to be a positive of the variable-time job—the higher income—is in many cases a detriment to spending time with family and training up a godly posterity.

Business owners are a case in point. In most situations they are not only the visionaries of their businesses but also the primary decision-makers. Though they usually have sufficient income to buy "freedom" by hiring others to do some of their work they are typically hesitant to do so for fear of losing control. They simply can't let go of the decision making, and as a result their time is not free—it is not their own. They are the ones with the cellular phones on their boats; they discuss business via the car phone on the way to the airport for a family ski trip. As the business succeeds and generates more income, the opportunities to grow increase and their freedom is reduced even more. As a result, even though they have more financial capital than ever, they have less time with their families.

Let us also consider the doctors and dentists, vocations that hold an esteemed position in the minds of most people. They typically generate significant income and appear to allow for a lot of discretionary time to be with their families. However, doctors are on call at night and on weekends, an arrangement that can put significant challenges on spending time with family, especially in the early years of the practice.

What about salespersons? Their income is a function of their own efforts, and typically the more time they spend at their jobs, the more income they can make. Therefore, the pressure to do more and more is acute.

The job seems to have no boundaries as to the time that can be spent working.

The point is that the vocations that tend to generate the greater incomes also tend to exert the greatest pressure on the person's time. If not handled properly, this pressure can steal the time necessary to raise a godly posterity. The vocations that put the least stress on the person's time tend to produce less income and put more stress on the financial side.

Vocations that tend to generate the greater incomes also tend to exert the greatest pressure on the person's time.

A final comment about overworking: Many persons may overwork, not because of the money, but because their identity and self-image are tied to what they do. We must recognize that our self-image is a function of who we are in Christ; it should not depend on our vocation. We need to keep our egos out of it and realize that God "resists the proud" (1 Pet. 5:5).

Regardless of your vocation, consider the following observations as you struggle to balance your work and your need for a margin of time for training your posterity:

1. Find a vocation you enjoy and are equipped for, then live within the income it provides.

It is your responsibility to work hard and well at what God has called and equipped you to do (see Col. 3:23), realizing that the income you generate is no surprise to

Him. He sovereignly ordains it through your employer or through the clients or sales He allows you to have in your business if you are self-employed.

2. If you are in a fixed-time job that has limited income, do not think you would be better off in a vocation that paid more money.

It may be easier for you to raise a godly posterity because of fewer time pressures than it would be for the person who has the variable-time job and greater income. Although less income may result in more financial pressures, we will see in the next chapter that income is often not the reason for financial pressures; lifestyle is. Therefore, control your lifestyle, live within your income, and be content in the vocation God has called and equipped you for.

3. Be aware of the different time demands at your family's different stages.

The needs and time demands are the greatest when the children are young; those demands usually subside somewhat through the teenage years and into college.

Let's look at how this works out practically. If you are starting a business and you do not have any children, project what your time commitments will be later in the business as you start a family. If the growth of the business reduces your time commitments, that is good. But if business growth will require more of your time exactly when your children need you, you may want the business to grow more slowly or stay smaller longer. If you are in one vocation and are considering switching to another, be careful to evaluate the impact of the change on your time. Also evaluate where you are in the different stages of your family's life. If the children are young, you may be better off waiting a few more years until they are teenagers to make the switch. Or if they are teenagers, you may want to wait until they graduate.

A friend of mine illustrates this challenge. He works for a huge corporation with a lot of career possibilities. He is newly married and right now he travels three to four nights a week at least twice a month. He makes a good income, is building a good pension, and enjoys a lot of nice perks. I have cautioned him, however, that travel will not be so glamorous after his children are born. I have encouraged him to project his career path for the next two to five years to see how his time commitments may balance with a family. If balance does not look possible, it may be better for him to look for another vocation now before the income and perks of the business make it too difficult to change. If he is not careful, he will be too far up the career ladder to get off but not far up enough to have flexibility over his time.

If you are in one vocation and are considering switching to another, be careful to evaluate the impact of the change on your time.

I know this concept of slowly climbing or getting off the ladder is a difficult one, especially given the ego of the man. My encouragement, however, is to remind him what really counts for eternity.

I must add a comment here lest you think I am leaving God out of this equation. What if God "calls" you to another vocation at what appears to be a wrong time, for example, when the new job would take you away from your children? Using 1 Corinthians 10:13 and 1 Thessalonians 5:24 as cornerstone passages, I am convinced that God is faithful and will not call you to do something He will not also give you the ability to handle. In this case, He will give you the ability and energy to stay balanced. It is hard, however, to fathom God's calling someone to a job that would dilute His ministry in people's (and children's) lives.

4. Do not be in a big hurry to retire and quit working. Extend your work horizon.

One of the biggest obstacles to keeping work in balance is the hurry-up-and-retire mentality. In our business we have found that regardless of how much money a person has, in most cases, he will continue to work.

One of the biggest obstacles to keeping work in balance is the hurry-up-and-retire mentality.

Work is good (see Gen. 2:5, 15), and it brings fulfillment. Man was created by God to work, and if he doesn't work he may be quite miserable, as this *Wall Street Journal* article by Jeff Tannenbaum illustrates:

> An attractive buy-out offer popped up and Mr. Gray sold out, thinking he'd never work again. "It was the great American dream of retiring." Trouble is, Dan Gray was soon climbing the walls. He found little to do but mow his lawn and visit Dan Enterprises as a consultant whose advice was usually ignored. "All of my friends were off working," he recalls. "There was nobody to play with." Within a year and a half, Mr. Gray started another T-shirt maker, Advance Industries, Inc., which he still runs. He had learned a lesson: "People who build companies can't get used to just stopping. It makes you crazy." In the lives of entrepreneurs, few periods are more stressful than that which Steven Berglas, a Boston psychotherapist, calls "harvesting time." Some business owners feel burned out in their jobs but hesitate to "harvest" because they have no idea of what to do next. Others sell, but grossly underestimate the personal adjustment problems they will face later even if they're rolling in money.[8]

You have your entire lifetime to work, and only twenty years to make the primary impact on your posterity. Therefore, *earn your income slowly.* Spread your earnings over a forty- to fifty-year period. You do not have to be a millionaire by the time you are forty and retire at fifty-five!

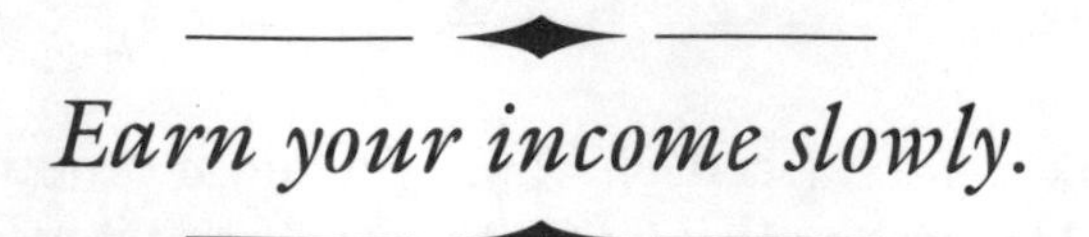

William Johnston of the Hudson Institute said, "Policymakers might want to encourage people to take more leisure earlier in life, then work longer later on or never really retire at all. Workers in their 30s or 40s could be granted sabbaticals to travel or raise children, drawing down some pension funds in exchange for working to age 70 or 75."[9] This surely seems like a great idea in light of the tension between family and work in the early years of one's life.

William Mattox, Jr., of the Family Research Council in Washington, D.C., comments:

> . . . the brawnpower to brainpower shift makes increasingly possible a long-overdue reordering of work and family responsibilities over the life cycle. Curiously, American families currently devote greater hours to paid work during the stage in life when they are most apt to have childrearing responsibilities and fewer hours (if any at all) than during the twilight years of life (between ages 55 and 70) when they are least apt to have dependent care duties. This peculiar distribution of work and family responsibilities (which, it should be noted, has become even more pronounced in recent years due to rises in maternal employment and early retirement) may have been justified in earlier days when young, strong backs were in greater demand than seasoned, sharp minds. But with recent economic shifts, along with the rise in average life expectancy, it no longer makes sense to order responsibilities in this way.[10]

One of the greatest causes of midlife crisis is the fact that many men work so hard and go so fast they accomplish all their goals by the time they reach forty. Then they wonder *What is next?* What is next is what they forgot. They forgot to spend time with their kids and wife and by then, in many cases, it is too late.

5. Only change vocations to better fulfill your purpose and maximize your time flexibility, not to make more money.

As Solomon said in Ecclesiastes, "He who loves silver will not be satisfied with silver; nor he who loves abundance, with increase. This also is vanity" (Eccles. 5:10).

A change in vocation will by necessity require a greater time commitment; you must invest time to learn the new job. This may be all right if the investment of additional time does not last too long and will result in more time, flexibility, and options later. However, many individuals change vocations in pursuit of more money only to find that the cost to the family was not worth it. Also, many times making the change takes so much emotional energy that the additional income is not worth the effort. We have only so much emotional energy; if we spend it all on job changes, we do not have any left to apply to raising our children.

This is not to say that you should not change vocations, only to caution you to weigh the cost. It may be that you would be better off waiting and earning less income at the old job until your children are at an age where a job change wouldn't be so disruptive to them in taking you away from them.

A friend of mine recently decided to change jobs. Although his motive was not more money, he underestimated the emotional cost. Not only were his financial pressures increased when he changed jobs, his time commitments increased as well. Now his wife needs to work because he is having trouble financially. This would not be a significant problem if the children were older, but they need Mom and Dad now—not in three to five years when less time and energy are demanded by the new job.

I also remember when I taught school fifteen years ago. I decided to change jobs, and one of the teachers commented that I could make a change relatively easily at that point because I had no children, but that it would be harder if I were further down the vocational road. I did not know what he meant then but I do now. It would have been difficult to spend the time necessary to start my financial-planning career if I had had young children. If that had been the case, I might have been better off staying in the lower-paying teaching job with less emotional and time pressures. This is not to discount following God's call about changing jobs. It is just that flexibility needs to be a high consideration.

6. If you are in a variable-time job, set your time parameters and do what you can do, then trust God to do what you cannot do.

If you are a salesperson, specify a reasonable number of hours you are going to devote to your work. Set an amount that will allow you to provide for your family's needs, and work hard during those hours; but when those hours are up, stop working and spend time with your family.

If you are in an unavoidable situation that requires you to spend a large block of time at work, try to make up for the overtime later through extended and relaxed times with the family. As an example, let me tell you about a tough week I had recently. I had three out-of-town trips in seven days, including four nights away from home. Since I knew this was coming, however, I planned to take some relaxed time with my family the week after the trip. I did not schedule any early-morning meetings so I could have breakfast with the kids and a cup of coffee with Julie. When work does get out of balance, *make plans to bring it back into equilibrium*. Put time with family in your business calendar book just as you do your work appointments. Plan to build in margin by coming home early or going in late a couple of days a week. This is a good discipline to develop.

Put time with family in your business calendar book just as you do your work appointments.

7. If you are in a vocation that is currently generating sufficient income, be careful to evaluate additional time spent to earn more income, especially if your children are young.

If you have the opportunity in your vocation to opt for less income or to freeze your income and get more time when the demands of your family are the greatest, consider doing it. Do not fall into the trap of thinking, *I'll work real hard now and make a lot of money and then I will spend time with the children*. Remember, the children's first ten years are the most critical. If you are making enough, the extra time may be more valuable than the extra money.

An article in *Money* magazine illustrated this point quite nicely. It said, "Once you've reached a certain level of comfort, the return on extra earnings begins to diminish—particularly if the extra work erodes your quality of life. . . . You may be able to improve your life by reducing spending."[11]

Here are some practical ways to implement this observation:

- Opt for a slower career path, and plan to work until you are 70 or 75. Although some corporations are not concerned about family and may label you as disloyal if you take this option, there seems to be more and more flexibility on this front. In today's economic environment, many companies are looking for creative ways to compensate employees other than with salary increases. Some of the ways they are doing this are by offering flexible time schedules, alternative work schedules, and more vacation time and personal days. Do not hesitate to negotiate with your employer.
- If you are the boss, consider reducing your income so you can hire someone to free up some of your time. For example, a friend of mine did not need the six-figure income he was making, so I suggested he use the extra income to hire some help. He did it and now has more time with his children at a very strategic time in their development.
- As a trade-off, opt for more vacation time instead of salary increases. I know of some Fortune 500 companies that allow employees to elect "vacation days" as part of their benefits package. The employee "buys" these days through reduced salary.

- Offer to work four-day weeks rather than five for 80 percent of your current salary.
- Offer to work six- or seven-hour days versus the traditional eight- to ten-hour days for less salary.

Of course, to successfully implement this observation it is important to make good financial decisions and control your lifestyle so you don't need to earn more and more money.

Balance Is the Key

As Charles Spurgeon once said, "All men must work, but no man should work beyond his physical and intellectual ability, nor beyond the hours which nature allots. No net result of good to the individual nor the race comes of any artificial prolonging of the day at either end. Work while it is day. When night comes, rest."[12]

Spurgeon was right. No good comes from overworking, especially when the cost of the overwork is the family. A recent article entitled "Beyond Success" by Rob Phillips showed that even the secular mind-set is starting to agree with the current thinking about balance:

> A young doctor cuts back his highly successful practice to spend more time with his wife and two children.
>
> An upward-bound executive declines a transfer from the community where she's put down roots.
>
> A business owner wears a beeper on his belt so his wife and children can reach him at any time.

> A senior lawyer derives satisfaction from helping disadvantaged families through his church, and adjusts his calendar accordingly.
>
> The solution, they say, is to redefine success.[13]

Phillips went on to quote Dr. Steven Berglas, a Boston-area psychotherapist and psychologist, who said, "There is no more direct route to self-esteem than climbing the ladder and reaching for the top—when pursued from a balanced perspective. . . . The entire materialism of the '80s has become politically incorrect. Now there is a window of opportunity to integrate meaning into the short-term self-interest that was characteristic of the last decade."[14]

We Christians should be at the forefront of this movement to balance life and integrate meaning into our lives. We must be prepared to handle the peer pressure of the world and even of some well-meaning Christians who will not understand us. "Why," they will wonder, "are you slowing down your climb up the ladder? Why didn't you take that job with more income? Why do you drive that old car and live in a smaller house?" The answer is that we look to the end of our lives and realize we must make the tough decisions *now*.

In the next chapter we will see that, not only must we earn our money with balance, but we must also make good financial decisions to have time to spend with our spouse and children.

For Further Reflection

1. List five vocations that would be considered variable-time jobs.

2. List five vocations that would be considered fixed-time occupations.

3. Do you agree that more income is typically generated by variable-time vocations? Why or why not?

4. Do you feel you are in a rush to retire? If so, would it be possible to slow down this rush? Would it cause you to lose your job? Do you have any creative options to accomplish this?

5. Is it possible in today's society to balance work and family? Why or why not?

7

WANTING IT ALL

FOUR MAJOR FINANCIAL DECISIONS THAT AFFECT ETERNITY

Too many people spend money they haven't earned to buy things they don't need to impress people they don't like.

Will Rogers

The rich rules over the poor, and the borrower becomes the lender's slave.

Proverbs 22:7 (NASB)

A gentleman went into a jewelry store to buy a Rolex watch (a symbol of prosperity and wealth). To pay for the watch he had to use three different credit cards. When the jeweler questioned, "Are you sure you can afford this?" the man replied, "I can't afford not to have it!" He was a living example of Will Rogers's famous statement. He was using money he didn't have to buy something he didn't need to impress people, most of whom he didn't even know.

It is easy to use our money to buy things. Consider the following:

> Mr. and Mrs. Thing are a very pleasant and successful couple. At least, that's the verdict of most people who tend to measure success with a "thingometer." When the "thingometer" is put to work in the life of Mr. and Mrs. Thing, the result is startling! There he is sitting down on a luxurious and very expensive thing, almost hidden by a large number of other things. Things to sit on, things to sit at, things to cook on, things to eat from, all shining and new. Things, things, things. Things to clean with and things to wash with and things to clean and things to wash. And things to amuse, and things to give pleasure and things to watch and things to play. . . .
>
> Anonymous

You may be asking, "Is there something wrong with using money to buy things?" The answer is no, but the issue is bigger than things. The issue is using our money *strategically* to ensure that we have time to spend on investing in our posterity. So the answer to the question, "How do you use your money to enhance your ability to balance your life?" is critical.

Four Major Financial Decisions That Affect Eternity

We are constantly bombarded with an unending assortment of things we are made to feel we can't live without. Most of us cannot resist the pressure. Before we know it we have bought all the latest gadgets, the newest vehicles, the nicest toys for our children, and the current fashions in clothes—and we wonder why the budget doesn't balance.

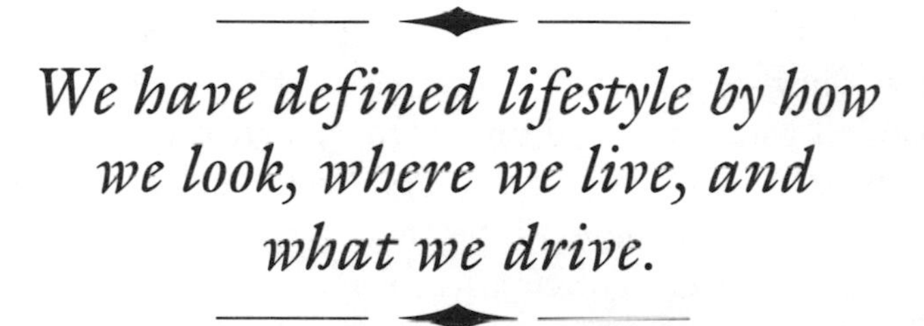

Carrie Teegardin described this in perfect clarity in her article "Load Too Heavy for Many" when she wrote,

> Some experts believe that the needs of a consumer economy have produced a new standard of living that people must work overtime to achieve. And it's a standard that Madison Avenue has been more than happy to reinforce.
>
> Some Americans still think they have to have a big house, two cars, state-of-the-art electronics and a nice vacation every year.
>
> They think they must work out three times a week at a nice health club, play golf once a week and send their kids to private school.[1]

We want to live like Mom and Dad when we are only a few years into our marriages, and we also want to "keep up with the Joneses." We have defined lifestyle by how we look, where we live, and what we drive. The problem is then compounded in that we typically use debt to fund our lifestyles. Let me illustrate what happens all too frequently.

Bill and Joan Wanted It All

Bill and Joan got married shortly after graduating from State University. Bill graduated with a degree in business management and Joan with a degree in nursing. They were excited when they both were able to get jobs in the same medium-sized city in the Midwest. With two incomes and no significant drains on their cash flow, they moved into their two-bedroom apartment with great anticipation for a wonderful future. They enjoyed their time together as newlyweds, eating out a lot and traveling on the weekends. Bill even planned a surprise ski trip as a special valentine gift to Joan.

After a few months of married life, however, Joan experienced some frustration with the apartment. She was not having any fun, she told Bill, because she was not able to decorate as she would like. It was not the same as if they had their own place. Bill agreed. After all, he would like to have a yard and some space for a shop. He had also been thinking about getting a motorcycle, and he'd need a garage to park it in.

They called Carla, a friend in the real estate business, and told her they would like to buy a house. In the meantime, Bill's five-year-old car, purchased when he was in college, gave him some problems, so he decided he might as well get another one. He traded it in for a brand-new, moderately priced sports car that only cost eighteen thousand dollars after the trade-in. He figured it was a good deal, especially since both he and Joan worked and could handle the monthly payments with no strain on their budget. Conveniently, too, the car loan was stretched over five years to make the monthly payments lower.

While Bill was car shopping Joan spent time with Carla, looking at houses. She found a place she really loved but knew it was a real financial stretch for them. "You and Bill should receive significant salary increases over the next several years," Carla pointed out, "so the monthly payments will eventually become less onerous on your budget." That made sense to Joan. "This is really my dream house," she told Bill.

Bill thought it over and agreed with Carla. Even though the payments would be tough, he felt he had potential in his job, and besides, he really liked the place too. It was even nicer than the one his parents lived in at the current time.

Bill and Joan moved into their dream house two days after their one-year apartment lease was up. As they moved their furniture and other household goods into the new home, they were astonished at how little room their furniture took up. Joan said, "Obviously, we need to get some more furniture." Over the next twelve months she and Bill spent a lot of time shopping for furniture and other items for the house. Bill also spent some time with a landscaper, fixing up the yard, and soon the garage housed a new lawn mower as well as the sports car and motorcycle.

When they realized in early June that Joan was pregnant, she was already two months along; a baby was due in January.

Although excited at first, Bill suddenly realized what this meant. Not only would they have another mouth to feed, which would cause an increase in their expenses, but what would he do if Joan could not go back to work? He had always figured they would have several years of both of them working so they could get some of their debts paid off before she got pregnant.

Bill and Joan found themselves in a quandary. It was doubtful that Bill's income could support their current lifestyle with the decisions they had made and the debt they had incurred. To Bill this meant at least one or two changes must occur. First, he would have to work harder and longer—potentially at two jobs—to try to make ends meet, which would leave him less time to spend building social and spiritual capital with his new family member. Second, Joan would have to go back to work and have less time with the baby. This, too, would have a negative impact on the building of social and spiritual capital.

Another solution existed, but it was not as obvious to Bill. Since he and Joan wanted to have time with their new and growing family, they could reduce their lifestyle. As Teegardin said, "If Americans accept the standard of living the middle class enjoyed a decade ago, some say, they could spend less time at work."[2] Easier said than done! Reducing one's lifestyle is incredibly difficult to do, especially to those who have gotten used to living a certain way (and used debt to fund that lifestyle).

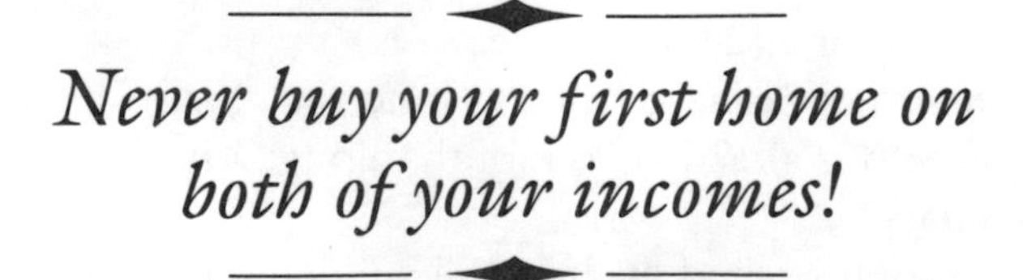

Before we look at some of the critical financial decisions we face and their impact on our time, I want to remind you that these principles do not just apply to young couples starting out. Indeed, some of our clients moved into their dream houses after their children were eight to twelve years old only to find that the additional debt they incurred put the same financial stress on them as it did on Joan and Bill. If these critical decisions are mishandled at any point in life, the potential exists for stress between work and family.

I recall an individual who wanted to change vocations twelve years into his career. His new job would allow him to do something he was better equipped for, and at the same time he would have more time to spend with his wife and children. He found, however, that this job would not pay him enough to support his current lifestyle and his current debt load. He said the job "only paid $60,000"! His financial decisions had gotten his expenses and his debt so high that he had to make $100,000 to support them. Do not let the magnitude of these numbers cause you to miss the point. Financial decisions are *critical* in maximizing your flexibility to balance work and family.

The critical decisions Bill and Joan faced also confront each of us—house, cars, lifestyle decisions, and investment decisions. As we analyze the impact of these decisions on our ability to balance family and work, some action steps become apparent.

1. The Bigger-House Decision

The house decision is the most critical financial decision most of us will make. Not only does the price of the house dictate our largest debt obligation, but the bigger and more costly the house, the greater the other expenses—utilities, property taxes, insurance, furnishings, repairs, and maintenance.

There is tremendous pressure to buy too much house for one's budget at two critical stages in our lives. The first occurs when we are just beginning our careers and families. Like Bill and Joan, we are tempted to buy more house than we can afford because we think we will be able to "earn" our way into it. In some cases, couples can do this without both spouses working. However, the risk of not being able to do so is too great, even if one's income might increase rapidly enough to support the stretch. Any marginal time a couple may have to spend with their children when they are young is consumed by working to make money to pay for the house. By the time they have worked their income up to a high enough level to create some breathing room in their budget the kids are already ten—and past the age when parents have the most influence on them.

We recommend that young couples do several things. First and most important, *never buy your first home on both of your incomes!* Make sure you buy a home that will work into your budget on the income of the husband only. Then when the wife gets pregnant, as Joan did, there won't be the pressure of having to go back to work after the baby is born. It is much easier to move up slowly in size and price than to move back. It is okay to start with a "starter home"! Yet young couples today want to skip the starter home and get to the dream-house stage. (Isn't it interesting that America is the only country where starter homes exist? The term implies the buyers are not going to stay there.)

Second, since many couples today are well educated and will be in the workplace early in their marriages, we recommend that the wife's net income (after taxes) be saved. Simply act as if it is not there and save it. This will allow you to buy more house using only the husband's income or to buy the same-sized house with a greater down payment, reducing the subsequent payments. If the husband's income will support payments on a $100,000 mortgage and you save $30,000, you will have two options. First, you could buy a bigger house and keep the $100,000 mortgage by applying the $30,000 to the down payment. Second, you could borrow only $70,000 by putting down $30,000 more on the same house. The lower borrowing will reduce the monthly payments, giving you more discretionary income and as a consequence more discretionary time.

Third, don't buy the lie that renting is always bad. Many times you are better off to rent longer so you can save a greater down payment and thereby reduce your mortgage payment which, in turn, maximizes your flexibility. (See Appendix B for a chart that analyzes buying versus renting.)

The second time there is great temptation to buy more house is about eight to fifteen years into a couple's work and marriage. Several things converge during this time frame to create what often seems like an acute need for a different (and usually larger) house. First, all the children have usually been born by this time. Not only are all the children on the scene, but they are growing and needing more room. At the same time the peer pressure to buy something nicer to ("keep up with the Joneses") is greatest on Mom and Dad. They have gotten their family and work off the ground and most of their friends have nicer places, so they begin to feel they deserve a new place too. The husband is typically approaching middle age, and the big, new house is the man's attempt to assuage his own ego in many cases. He feels he deserves his dream house after working so hard for all these years.

It is interesting to note that just when the family budget is usually beginning to get some breathing room (as a result of Dad's increasing salary over the years and living in the older, less-expensive house) a couple decides to get right back under the pile. They buy the big house and stretch their finances all over again; then they spend the rest of their children's formative years (the next eight to fifteen years) under financial pressure again.

One of the best things a couple can do to balance work and family during the formative years of their children's lives is to live in the older, smaller house a few years longer. Instead of having such a great percentage of their earnings earmarked for the house, more discretionary funds can be invested in family activities such as vacations, ball games, and the like. Also, it may be that Dad could opt for smaller salary increases and more vacation time, as mentioned in the last chapter.

One of the best things a couple can do to balance work and family during the formative years of their children's lives is to live in the older, smaller house a few years longer.

I also recommend that you avoid succumbing to the mirage principle. Most of the big houses that "the Joneses" are living in are not paid for. As a matter of fact, there is probably less equity in their homes than you have in your older, smaller home. If they have any glitch in their income (such as the husband losing his job or having to take a pay cut or the wife becoming unable to work) then the whole thing disappears. They lose it all.

Many couples I know are house poor; they work themselves to a frazzle to make the monthly payments and keep the place up, and there is no money and time left to do anything else. And the travesty is that children do not care where they live! They just want Mom and Dad to be around and have some emotional energy to give them.

I will never forget the comment of a friend's wife who lived in a beautiful 6,500-square-foot home on five beautiful acres. "Russ," she said, "I enjoyed our 2,500-square-foot home much more than this one. It was much easier to decorate, and the kids were much closer together. Here there is so much room we hardly see each other. All the kids have their own rooms. It's a nice house, but it is not a home."

This is not to say one should never buy a bigger house. However, consideration should be given to purchasing a new house only when adequate savings have been accrued so the family's monthly outgo will not be changed. For example, let's assume I live in a $100,000 house with a $70,000 mortgage and I can handle the payments easily on my current income. If, over an eight- to fifteen-year period, I am able to save $50,000, then I could choose to buy a $150,000 house. I could put my additional $50,000 into a new house and effectively keep my payments the same. Obviously, a more expensive house will have some additional costs, but the biggest outlay is the mortgage. It follows, then, that if you can pay cash for the house, the size is irrelevant. What is relevant is maximizing your flexibility and options.

The second part of my recommendation would be to only change houses if it will enhance the environment you want for your family (and not take away from it). Will the new house be a home? Or will it be just a house because you are never there?

Parental Pressure

Many times the prior generation places subtle—and in some cases not so subtle—pressure on the current generation to look a certain way. I have heard of numerous situations where young mothers are encouraged by their parents to work. "After all," the parents say, "you've got a good mind. How are you going to get ahead if you don't work?" Or they might make comments to the couple such as, "When are you going to get a new car (or a new house)?" or "Don't you think the children could use some name-brand clothes?" or "Why don't you go on vacation at that nice place on the beach?"

I believe this occurs, in many cases, because the parents want their adult children to look a certain way. They do not want their children in a starter home because it does not look good enough to the parents' friends. They are embarrassed if their children and grandchildren are driving a ten-year-old car. A young couple needs to be aware of these motivations, and the parents of this young couple need to let them begin as they, themselves, probably did.

If you are like these parents, stop! Do not discourage the young couple from living in the smaller home and driving the older car a little longer. The world they are raising your grandchildren in is more urban and less agrarian and has pressures you did not have. The schools, the churches, and the society at large are much more anti-God than they were thirty to fifty years ago. I read in a recent poll that "81 percent of the adults in this country believe that it is tougher for children to grow up in America today than it was when they were kids."[3]

James Dobson described it this way:

> The environment in which children are being raised has changed dramatically in the past few years, creating new anxieties for mothers and fathers. Unspeakable dangers haunt our schools and streets that were almost unheard of a generation ago. Yesterday's families didn't worry much about drive-by shootings, illegal drugs, sexual molesters and kidnappers. When I was a kid in the early 1950's, my folks were more concerned about a disease called polio than all sources of violence combined. As a 10-year-old, I moved freely around my home town. If I was a half-hour late coming home for dinner, the Dobson household was not seized by panic. But now the culture has changed! Now we worry about our kids playing in the front yard. . . . Unfortunately, the risks to today's children are not limited to physical threats. Parents must also worry about the culture and how it impacts the hearts and minds of their precious kids . . . the struggle to protect their children from the culture goes far beyond junk food and celebrities pushing sneakers. It has become a daunting task to shield the younger generation from "safe-sex" instruction in school, from profane and sacrilegious language in the neighborhood, from immorality and violence on television, from homosexual and lesbian propaganda and from wickedness and evil of every stripe.[4]

This deterioration of society means your adult children's time with their children is potentially more critical than ever—and more difficult to come by. Encourage them to be in the fight. Don't pressure them, especially in the house and car area. Money and image are secondary to time with posterity.

Buying a car, the second critical financial decision, and buying a home are not problems in themselves. When these two items require the use of debt, however, they can create problems because the more debt a couple take on, the less flexibility they have. It is my observation that parents preoccupied with debt problems will not invest adequate time and spiritual resources in their children, which assures that they will not have the spiritual capability to manage the financial resources that may be left to them.

2. The New-Car Decision

Bill and Joan also made a couple of mistakes in their car decision. First, they did not pay cash; instead they took out a five-year note. This enabled them to handle the payments, but ensured that they will probably owe more than the car is worth in a couple of years. This problem will be accentuated because of the second mistake they made. They bought a car that will be dysfunctional for a growing family in another year or two and, as a consequence, will necessitate buying another car. As a result they will need to sell their first car and probably will lose money on it. Buying ***new*** cars frequently is a good way to keep one's finances on the edge by keeping cash flow tight.

What I recommend is very simple: Pay cash for your cars if at all possible, buy used instead of new cars, and plan to drive your cars at least ten years. Fifty percent of all cars ten years old and older are still on the road. The older the car gets, the less the taxes and insurance. Maintenance costs increase, but they are usually significantly less than the annual interest cost on a new-car loan. Used cars allow you to take advantage of the immediate depreciation that occurs in the first year or two of a car's "life."

Julie and I bought a twenty-thousand-dollar car that was two years old for ten thousand dollars, and we're now in the eighth year with that car. If you cannot pay cash immediately but will plan to drive your car ten years or longer, you will be able to pay cash for your next car. How? If your current car payment is three hundred dollars per month and your car is paid off in five years, keep setting aside the three hundred per month in a savings account for the next five years. You will have accumulated eighteen thousand dollars plus interest, and this should allow you to pay cash for the next car. The key to reversing the debt cycle is driving the older car longer.

Pay cash for your cars if at all possible, buy used instead of new cars, and plan to drive your cars at least ten years.

I do not know anyone, myself included, who does not think it would be nice to have a new car. But driving the older car longer really does work to enhance freedom and options. The following letter, received in our office, shows what happens when this principle is put into practice:

You stated that cars rarely appreciate in value and rather depreciate. Secondly, car purchases are really ego decisions, not financial decisions. I wanted to share with you the story of my implementation of one of your financial strategies based upon these two points.

Returning to Atlanta, the lessons you taught were still fresh in my mind when I noticed that my next-door neighbor had a very old car parked in her driveway. It was the ugliest color of yellow that I had seen—faded canary like a banana!

I asked about it and discovered that it was bequeathed to my neighbor from her Great Aunt Mary in Chicago. It was a 1966 Plymouth Valiant with 106,000 original miles on it. No kidding—just driven to church on Sundays!

For whatever reason, a thought was planted in my mind that this was an opportunity to test my motives. Had I bought into the ego syndrome of auto consumption? Yes, I had. I had owned six sports cars in almost as many years and most of them were bought new.

So I asked my wife what she thought about me selling my Saab Turbo and offering to buy my neighbor's car. Although she initially thought I was only kidding, my persistence conveyed my seriousness. She also had heard your presentation and was willing to support me in my decision. So I sold the Saab in a week, paid off the remaining loan, bought the Valiant, and put the savings in the bank.

The cost of the car? $300! It came complete with Aunt Mary's driving gloves and her hat in the rear window. So that I would always be aware of the temperature, the car also included a window thermometer from a Chicago funeral home that was attached to the driver's-side window (I guess she visited there often).

Now I bet you are saying that was probably not a wise decision because of the potential repairs that I would have to make. Or there might be a lot of downtime and inconvenience. This is where I truly believe God was involved in orchestrating all of this. I have spent less than $350 in repairs in 2 years and I can have her repaired at the local gas station or garage! I can do without those high-priced European service departments.

Was it a good decision? I believe it was. First, I broke the desire that I had for expensive cars. Secondly, I was freed from caring where I parked the car. Previously, I was always conscious of parking so that the doors would not be dented by others getting out of their cars. Third, I was totally debt free and was earning interest as opposed to paying it. I was a lender, not a borrower. Fourth, I needed that money a few months later in that I was accepted into the Harvard Business School and would need every dollar I could garner for tuition. Finally, it was fun driving Aunt Mary, the name my friends teasingly called the car. It was a conversation piece and a testimony of good stewardship.

Sure, it is a hassle only being able to drive 55 miles an hour. Aunt Mary [as we call the car now] just can't make it any faster. She is also quite hot in the summer because she doesn't have air conditioning, but that's okay—I just sweat a little bit in the afternoons. These are two small prices to pay for the rewards I have received.[5]

If you can pay cash for your car, it really does not matter what you drive as long as you are not neglecting your charitable giving to the Lord. If you can afford a BMW or Lexus, it is okay if you decide, as a couple, that you want to spend your money this way.

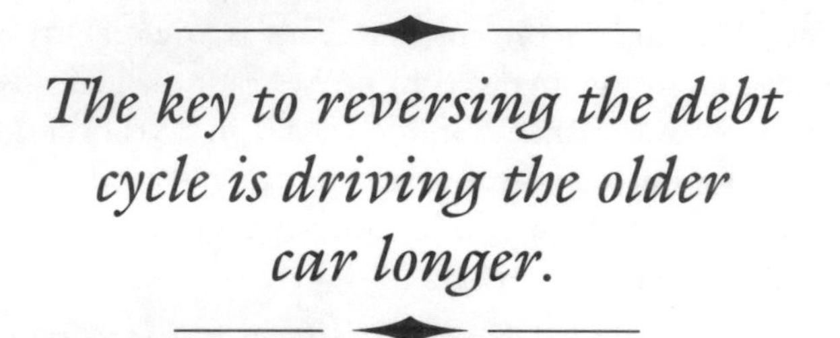

The key to reversing the debt cycle is driving the older car longer.

Yes, it is possible to make good decisions regarding cars. It will not be easy, but the rewards are worth it.

3. Lifestyle Decisions

Another mistake people make is to develop expensive habits and hobbies. Although these can seem affordable early in a marriage when there are two incomes, they can become tremendous drains on the budget later on. For instance, Bill and Joan's habits of eating out and frequently taking expensive vacations cost a lot of money. Sometimes couples will continue these habits and pay for them with a credit card. Instead, their attitude toward their lifestyle must change. They should tell themselves, "If we cannot pay cash, we will not do it."

Furnishing and decorating a home is also a lifestyle issue. Are you willing to wait to furnish the house until you have the cash, or will you go into debt to get it fixed up as fast as you can?

Julie and I heard of a couple who had a beautiful old home decorated all in white, who only allowed their children to play in the basement because they did not want them messing up the house. I wonder what kind of impact that will have on their posterity!

One final lifestyle choice is the issue of education. Many people are concerned about their children's education—and rightfully so. This concern, however, many times leads to the pressure to send the children to private elementary and high schools as well as to the finest colleges. On the surface this seems like good thinking. However, I have seen many mothers go back into the work force to pay the child's private-school tuition or many dads work a second job for the same reason. I often wonder if their emotional energy might not be better spent on training their children; maybe saving the money and using their time to home-school the children rather than work would be a more effective way to educate them. We must remember that we want our children to be ***knowledgeable***, but ***wisdom*** is more important. We, as parents, impart wisdom to our children, and that takes time! Just as children don't care where they live, they don't care where they are educated as long as you are around and involved with their training.

I would rather have smaller raises now and more vacations when my children are young than have it the other way around. I will have a lot of time to work when they are in college and when they have careers of their own. Also, because I understand the principle of long-time horizons (which means not being in a hurry to retire), I am not under pressure to generate more income now so I can set aside a lot each year for retirement. I tend to invest some of my "retirement money" in my children now, using some of these funds for family memory builders, for trips to the ballpark, and for paying off debt.

In this section we have looked at various lifestyle decisions about homes, cars, material possessions, and our children's education that can have a negative impact on a couple's ability to maximize their time and increase their margin. Before moving on let's look at a principle that should make it easier to resist the urge to accumulate more and more things in order to keep up with and look like everybody else: The principle is one of *limited sphere*.

The Principle of Limited Sphere

Julie, the boys, and I typically travel cross-country every summer on our way to Colorado or Kansas. In each small town we pass through we observe the nice as well as the not-so-nice parts of town. It is never difficult to spot the home of the wealthiest people in town. We have observed that in each town one or two families appear to sit atop the socioeconomic ladder. They and maybe even some around them are undoubtedly impressed with their status and position in the community. But you and I don't even know them. Put that same home in a typical north Atlanta subdivision, for example, and it is nothing special. And so it goes.

Hundreds and thousands of people all across America have grand homes, ranches, and buildings. Most of those people we will never know about. And most will never know what you and I have either.

As I reflect on this concept, I conclude that the sphere of people who ever really know what we have materially is incredibly small. At most there might be seventy-five to one hundred people in my sphere who know what I have materially (what kind of car I drive, where my house is, what is in my house, what kind of clothes I wear, and so on). As a result it doesn't seem to make much sense to strap myself financially buying things to impress such a small group.

The choice seems to be between investing our money in materialism to impress a limited sphere of people or investing our money in our posterity, who can change their world for the better and consequently impact an unlimited sphere.

No matter what a person has—a private jet, a mansion in the country, a lake home, a yacht—someone else always has more. On top of that we all end up the same, since we can take nothing with us. King Solomon, one of the wealthiest men who ever lived, observed, "As he came from his mother's womb, naked shall he return, to go as he came; and he shall take nothing from his labor which he may carry away in his hand" (Eccles. 5:15).

The only thing we leave is our mark on people and our posterity. The choice seems to be between investing our money in materialism to impress a limited sphere of people or investing our money in our posterity, who can change their world for the better and consequently impact an unlimited sphere. Think about it. If you train your children and they train theirs and they all impact others for Christ, the influence spreads. Similarly, think about the money you give to charitable causes. It, too, can have a worldwide impact.

4. Investment Decisions

I have seen many cases where couples attempting to "make it big" took inordinate risks with their investments only to lose their money. Many times the motivation for the risk was good: to make a lot of money so they would have time and flexibility to spend with family.

If such investments work out, great. But what if the investment turns sour? I believe the risk is too great. Very rarely do people make large enough returns on their investments that they become financially independent. I've found that financial independence occurs by spending less than one makes over a long period of time, not from gaining big returns on investments.

I discourage taking undue risk with your investment dollars until your children are at least eighteen. Instead, I encourage you to invest very conservatively to ensure that you do not lose your investments. You can take all the risks you want when the children are older and no longer require as much of your time. Besides, you will surely be wiser by then!

In Appendix C I suggest four specific steps you can take to manage your money more efficiently. The worksheets included in Appendix C will help you apply the ideas to your own finances.

A Personal Example

Julie and I decided many years ago that our motivation for managing our finances was not to have more money so we could retire or just to have more money. Instead, we agreed that our motivation would be to manage our finances correctly and wisely to increase our options and flexibility, to buy time, to reduce our pace, and to increase margin.

We have been in our home eleven years, and many times we have been tempted to take on debt and get a place we would really like (our "dream spot"). After all, we rationalize, the kids could enjoy it; if we wait until we can easily afford to buy it, the children will likely be grown.

But then I consider how nice it is not to have the debt pressures a new home would bring. I think about the fact that we have discretionary income that enables us to go on family vacations and create special memories. I am grateful that we can go out to eat or that I can buy some special things for Julie without using a credit card. We are glad that Julie can be a full-time mother and pour her emotional energy into our boys during these very formative years. We think about these things, and we stay put. If God blesses us financially and we could move without losing any of these benefits, we might do it, but not before those conditions are met.

Our cars are six and eight years old; the paint is starting to look bad on one and the other has a dent, but that is okay. We could use a van because the children are getting bigger, but we will not buy one until we can pay cash. We are on the ten-year plan, so we may be crowded for another four years. I do not think the children will be any worse off for being a little crowded. As a matter of fact, we were crowded in our little Volkswagen before we traded it, and the kids still miss it!

Finally, Julie and I are motivated to make good decisions financially because we realize that what we are buying is a rare commodity: time. We can either use our money to buy things that will not last (a bigger house, more toys, more stuff), or we can invest in our posterity, which will last. In the next chapters we will look at how we can use the time we buy when we make good financial decisions.

For Further Reflection

1. How does debt affect both work and family?

2. What lifestyle habits, if any, did you establish early in your marriage that have had an impact on your financial situation?

3. Do you agree with the thoughts on education funding expressed in this chapter? Why or why not?

4. What pressures, if any, have you felt from your parents in the financial area? What pressures have you put on your married children if you have them?

5. Do you have a financial plan that would help you balance work and family? If so, is it helping? If not, why not?

Part Three

How to Use Your Money More Effectively

8

Train Up a Child

Building Our Posterity's Spiritual Capital

I want to live one day over. With my children young again. An ordinary day. I have so much to tell them.

The Estate Sale video,
White Lion Pictograph Productions

And these words which I command you today shall be in your heart; you shall teach them diligently to your children, and shall talk of them when you sit in your house, when you walk by the way, when you lie down, and when you rise up.

Deuteronomy 6:6–7

We had just pulled into the garage when my first-born, Clark, made another angry response to the third-born, Chad. As we got out of the car I told Clark I wanted to talk with him. We proceeded to talk a bit about how anger does not please God (James 1:19) and how our words are to be kind and gentle and edifying, not unwholesome and coarse (see Col. 4:6; Eph. 4:29 and 5:4). We talked about his need to ask God to forgive him for the sin of anger (1 John 1:9) and to restore the relationship with his brother.

All these ideas and hundreds more are part of the fabric of spiritual capital we want to weave into our children's lives. That is why we need so much time. "There is so much to tell them," as the line in *The Estate Sale* video so poignantly states.

We also have so much we need to model for them—especially in the spiritual capital area. In this chapter, we will look at four essential building blocks of the spiritual foundation for children. Remember, the spiritual foundation we are laying includes an understanding of biblical absolutes and truths, of how to come to Christ, of God's character and attributes, of how to walk in faith and to trust God, and biblical principles of money management, childrearing, and husband/wife relationships. Spiritual capital is using the absolute truths of God's Word to determine right from wrong and good from evil.

The four building blocks—a global perspective; the training of trials and failure; the three biblical principles of giving; and work, church, and a heart for God—are by no means an exhaustive list. As a matter of fact, this is a rather short list that will deal with only a few areas that relate most directly to finances. I hope these will serve as an impetus for you to work on your foundation.

1. A Global Perspective

We must help our posterity see the world beyond this country. Thirteen years ago Julie and I had the opportunity to travel to Africa. That trip had a tremendous impact on our perspective of money and things. We lived in an apartment at the time of the trip, and we had frequently bemoaned the fact that we did not have a house. Also, since our budget was tight, we did not have the luxury to go out to eat very often or to buy the latest fashions.

After two weeks in Africa our apartment looked luxurious in comparison to the mud and, in many cases *manure*, huts in which many Africans lived. Just being able to eat what we wanted when we wanted with a *cold* glass of water from our refrigerator seemed great. And suddenly our older cars did not seem to be such bad transportation after all. In Africa we had seen the alternative—walking and donkeys, for example.

Our children need the same experience. They need to be exposed to the big world God has created, the different people He has created, and the different situations in which these people live. That exposure should expand their horizons and give them a greater appreciation of what they have and take their focus off money, things, and materialism. Having the name-brand clothes and the nicest car should not seem quite so important to them.

But you do not have to go to Africa to get a new perspective. A visit to the inner city of any major city in the United States should also change your perspective on needs, wants, and desires. Once a year Julie and I help the boys go through their toys and clothes to share with the less fortunate in our city. We then spend a day delivering these items and seeing how others live. We are prayerful that God will use this exposure to help our boys take their focus off materialism and instead put it on Him and what is going on in His world.

If our children are ever to correctly handle money, they need to have a perspective beyond their needs, wants, and desires. They must have a perspective on others' needs and on giving. We must help them be stewards, not consumers.

Pond water that doesn't move can become stale and stagnant and eventually polluted. A river, on the other hand, keeps moving; it is fresh and clear as long as no trash is dumped in it. It is the same with our lives. If we share the financial capital we have, we take the first step in being a steward. So I must not only expose my children to the needs around them, but also let them see me using my financial capital to meet those needs. They need to see me exercising stewardship, which is defined by Ron Blue as "the use of God-given resources to accomplish God-given goals."

If our children have everything they want, how can they learn to be dependent on God?

If we are to build the foundation of spiritual capital into our posterity, we must invest some of our current financial capital in experiences that give them this global perspective. We may have less financial capital at the end of our lives if we spend five thousand to ten thousand dollars to take our children to Africa or Russia now, but the return on the spiritual capital will be worth it. Or what about having a missionary from Africa in your home during the next missions conference in your area? It may only cost you an additional meal or two!

A global view helps our children understand the difference between the temporal and eternal (see 2 Cor. 4:18). If their focus is always on their own temporal needs and comfort rather than God's eternal perspective, they will find it very difficult to handle any financial capital they may receive in a nonconsumptive way. Julie and I plan to make this investment as soon as our children are old enough to gain the global perspective hoped for from the trip.

2. The Training of Trials and Failures

Trials will also enhance our posterity's spiritual foundation. The Bible is very clear that challenges and difficulties are God's method of training, teaching, and growing us to maturity in Him. The following verses depict this clearly:

> Count it all joy when you fall into various trials, knowing that the testing of your faith produces patience. (James 1:2–3)
>
> In this you greatly rejoice, though now for a little while, if need be, you have been grieved by various trials, that the genuineness of your faith, being much more precious than gold that perishes, though it is tested by fire, may be found to praise, honor, and glory at the revelation of Jesus Christ. (1 Pet. 1:6–7)
>
> Now no chastening seems to be joyful for the present, but grievous; nevertheless, afterward it yields the peaceable fruit of righteousness to those who have been trained by it. (Heb. 12:11)

Despite these scriptural directives, most parents find it difficult to let their children experience trials. Often, we overwork to earn more money so we can insulate them from difficulty. When they are young we buy them designer clothes so they can fit in and avoid peer pressure and ridicule that might come if they look different. When they get older we make sure they have a nice car so they are popular. We buy video games, televisions for their rooms, and state-of-the-art toys. We spend our money, many times using debt, to help our posterity have it easy, comfortable, and pleasurable.

It appears that the easier we make it for our children and the more comfortable they have it, the less chance they have of being great for God.

Think about the meaning of each of those words. *Ease* is defined as "freedom from labor, exertion, pain, annoyance; freedom from difficulty in great labor." Do we let our children suffer a little, or do we make it too easy for them? Do we turn up the air conditioning when it is a little too warm for them, clean their rooms when they forget, buy a riding lawn mower when the old one gets a little hard to push, and excuse them from taking out the garbage because they do not feel like doing it?

The definition of *comfort* is "to satisfy bodily wants and to free from all cares and anxieties." Do we teach our children to make do with what they have, or do we quickly move to fix the problem to free them from any anxiety?

Do we let them drop out of a sport if they do not like it or not do a speech at school because they are afraid?

Finally, the definition of *pleasure* is "doing what one wants; to experience good and delight as opposed to pain." Does my world revolve around my children? Do I always allow them to do what they want, or do they have to learn to adapt to others around them? Are there times they need to be flexible and cannot do all that they want? Do we teach our children to be still and quiet in church or the doctor's office? Do we take them with us shopping or to visit a friend, or do we get a baby-sitter so we do not have to train them to adapt and fit into our schedule? We need to be careful not to allow our children to be "lovers of pleasure rather than lovers of God" (2 Tim. 3:4).

If our children have everything they want, how can they learn to be dependent on God? As a matter of fact, ease may blind them to their need for God. In Daniel 4:4 (NASB), we read that Nebuchadnezzar "was at ease in my house and flourishing in my palace." He experienced comfort and pleasure. But it led to a pride and independence that caused him to forget God. In Amos 6:1 we read, "Woe to you who are at ease in Zion, and trust in Mount Samaria."

Of course parents want to make life easier for their children; on the surface, that is a normal, positive desire. However, overworking to buy the things to make life easier for children is negative. As a matter of fact, it appears that the easier we make it for our children and the more comfortable they have it, the less chance they have of being great for God.

J. K. Gresset said, "God prepares great men for great tasks by great trials."[1] A. W. Tozer added, "It is doubtful whether God can bless a man greatly until he has hurt him deeply."[2] Could we be crippling our children with the very things we are trying to do for them? We should be pursuing character and not comfort in our posterity. I agree with Randy Alcorn's sentiments:

> It is one thing to provide for our children, but quite another to smother them in things until they turn into self-indulgent materialists. An alarming number of children from Christian homes develop a basic identity as consumers rather than disciples. They grow up endlessly grasping for dolls, robots, plastic ponies, and everything else a production-oriented society can offer. Children raised in such an atmosphere—and that now includes most children in the United States—are often afflicted with the disease David McKenna calls *affluenza*. Affluenza is a strange malady that affects the children of well-to-do parents. Though having everything money can buy, the children show all of the symptoms of abject poverty—depression, anxiety, loss of meaning, and despair for the future. Affluenza accounts for an escape into alcohol, drugs, shoplifting, and suicide among children of the wealthy. It is most often found where parents are absent from the home and try to buy their children's love.[3]

Scripture is very clear that one of the greatest detriments to following God is independence. Our material possessions and money may make us independent and thus less dependent on God. And in giving our children everything money can buy we may cause them to lose a potentially close relationship with God. R. C. Sproul, the founder of Ligonier Ministries and a noted Bible scholar, wrote:

> Scripture tells us again and again that tribulation is a means by which we are purified and driven to a deeper dependence upon God. There is a long-range benefit

> to us that we would presumably lose were it not for the pain we are called to endure for a season. This is what Paul is teaching in Romans 8:18. Conversely, pleasure can be a narcotic and seductive; the more we enjoy it and the more we experience it, the less we see our dependence upon God's mercy and forgiveness. Pleasure can be not so much an angel in disguise as a devil in disguise to lead us into ultimate ruin. That's why we must be extremely careful, practically speaking, in pursuing too much pleasure lest we lose sight of our ultimate need for the mercy of God.[4]

Maybe this realization will make it easier to slow down and balance life rather than be in a hurry to earn more and more money. I hope you are as challenged as I am to be careful how I use my money in the lives of my children. After all, "He who loves pleasure will be a poor man" (Prov. 21:17).

If you struggle financially, take heart, for you may be more prosperous than you thought. You may find it easier to help your children learn to be dependent on God than the person who has a lot of income and discretionary money.

Therefore, if you struggle financially, take heart, for you may be more prosperous than you thought. You may find it easier to help your children learn to be dependent on God than the person who has a lot of income and discretionary money. If you do have a lot of money, realize the challenge you have to use your money wisely.

3. Three Biblical Principles—Giving, Work, and Church

Another key to developing spiritual capital in our children is to help them have a biblical basis for various issues of life. They need to see life through the grid of God's Word. Although a myriad of issues are discussed in Scripture (including relationships, leadership, investments, marriage, divorce, and others) three relate specifically to our topic: giving, work, and church.

Our children need to understand the principle of *giving* in addition to just saving and spending. We have tried to implement this in our children's lives at a very early age with three banks. One bank is for spending, one is for saving, and one is for giving. Their allowance must be put in all three banks. We want them to understand that all they have comes from God and some must be given to acknowledge His ownership. Many of the financial problems we face today in this country, as evidenced by the debt load of most families, are because we are a society of greedy people rather than givers. Our children should learn to share and give, especially financially.

Children also must understand that God commands us to *work*, and that if we do not work we do not generate the income necessary to provide for our families.

However, we have to keep our work in balance so we will not be a poor model for our children. Work is not more important than they are or more important than time with God. We will discuss this principle in greater detail later.

Finally, our work should be kept in balance so we have time to focus on the *church* and the *world*. As discussed in Chapter 6, it is not enough just to balance work and family; part of that balance includes attending church and being involved in evangelism and discipleship. I must manage my finances correctly to have time to model an involvement in the world as well as the church. There is no better way children can learn these important values than to see them modeled by their parents.

I might add that the form our involvement in the church and the world will take looks different at different ages of our kids' lives. Before Julie and I had children we were very active in the church, leading a Sunday school class and discipleship groups. After the children came along we discipled couples in our home and cut down on the number of formal meetings and committees we participated in. With children prone to ear infections, we found we had to drop out of the Sunday school and do Sunday school-type activities in the home. As the children get older, we can get more involved again. The important thing is that our children see us actively involved in some way in God's plan for the world: "Go therefore and make disciples of all the nations, baptizing them in the name of the Father and of the Son and of the Holy Spirit, teaching them to observe all things that I have commanded you; and lo, I am with you always, even to the end of the age" (Matt. 28:19–20).

The only way to do this is to keep our finances in order so we have time to focus on these areas in addition to our families. Our financial capital also should be used (invested) to create an environment that will promote and enhance spiritual capital. Therefore, you might choose to invest some money in attending Christian family camps where you can vacation as a family and learn some spiritual values. This may cost more than other vacations, but it may be worth the extra financial cost. The same is true for having your child go on a short-term mission project. If you can invest in vision trips, Christian camps, and Christian videos for your children, these may enhance their spiritual development. If you do not have the money, do not feel that it is a detriment to your children, for most spiritual values are taught by parents spending time with children.

4. A Heart for God

To build spiritual capital we can help our children learn to have a heart for God. There are two ways to do this. First, they should observe a calling in our lives that is bigger than what we are doing vocationally. They should observe that our lives are purposeful and focused on God's plan for us. It is not that we go to work for the sake of working, but rather that our work is what we do to accomplish God's bigger purpose for us.

I sense in my own life that this concept of posterity and prosperity is the message God has given me to share with the world. Therefore, as I travel, speak, and write, I explain to the boys what I am doing and why I am doing it. I pray that this wholehearted devotion to a purpose will awaken imitation in them at some point in the future.

In Chapter 7, I shared Billy Graham's statement in which he said he spent more time than he would have liked away from family. His son, Franklin, rebelled for a time, but now Franklin has come around and follows God's calling on his life. It seems that Billy Graham's wholehearted devotion to God's call on his life eventually had an impact on Franklin.

For all of our fast-paced progress, there is no "drive-through window" for knowing God. It requires purposeful meditation.

Second, our children need to see us praying, studying our Bible, having a daily quiet time, and talking about God as we walk by the way, as we rise up and as we sit down. During the last presidential election, we sat around the table after dinner and discussed how God sovereignly controls kings and rulers and that we could trust Him regardless of the outcome. This helped the children see that God is relevant in all issues of life.

As our children see the relevancy of God in our lives, we pray that they will begin to turn their hearts toward God and His way. We cannot teach our children to have a heart for God if all they ever see us doing is rushing off to work and never having time to discuss spiritual issues with them. We cannot teach them if we don't know God and develop a heart for God ourselves.

For all of our fast-paced progress, there is no "drive-through window" for knowing God. It requires purposeful meditation. J. I. Packer, in his classic book *Knowing God*, wrote,

> Meditation is the activity of calling to mind, thinking over, dwelling on, and applying to oneself the various things that one knows about the works, ways, purposes, and promises of God. It is an activity of holy thought, consciously performed in the presence of God, under the eye of God, by the help of God, as a means of communion with God. Its purpose is to clear one's mental and spiritual vision of God and to let His truth make its full and proper impact on one's mind and heart. It is a matter of talking to oneself about God and oneself; it is, indeed, often a matter of arguing with oneself, reasoning oneself out of moods of doubt and unbelief into a clear apprehension of God's power and grace.[5]

We cannot meditate without time! We must buy time and margin to be able to pray, study, meditate, and read in order to have something to pass on to our posterity. We need to be on guard for hurry and a too-fast pace that can kill these disciplines and render us empty—with no heart for God and nothing to share with our children.

Of course there are countless other components that build a spiritual foundation in our children. Areas such as absolutes versus situational ethics, how to pray, faith, discipline, the fruits of the spirit, and the importance of church attendance (Heb. 10:24–25). All of these absolutes, however, just reinforce this point: We must balance work and family in order to have time to focus emotional energy on these issues. How you go about building these ideas into your posterity is up to you, but I hope you are convinced now that money and the pursuit of it can, in many cases, only hurt this effort. Spiritual training must be caught *and* taught.

We must buy time and margin to be able to pray, study, meditate, and read in order to have something to pass on to our posterity. We need to be on guard for hurry and a too-fast pace that can kill these disciplines and render us empty—with no heart for God and nothing to share with our children.

For Further Reflection

1. What steps are you taking to build the spiritual foundation of your children?

2. What are some additional spiritual truths you believe your children should learn?

3. In what ways could you invest your money to enhance this area?

4. Do you have a calling that is bigger than what you do every day that your children will observe?

5. What are your written goals for your children in each of these areas—spiritual, intellectual, physical, and social?

6. Are you spending time with God to grow spiritually so you have spiritual values and principles to pass on to your children?

9

A Good Name Is Better Than Riches

Building Our Posterity's Social Capital

Good character is more to be praised than outstanding talent. Most talents are, to some extent, a gift. Good character, by contrast, is not given to us. We have to build it piece by piece—by thought, choice, courage, and determination.

John Luther

You can't leave character in a trust account. You can't write your values into the will. You can't bank traits like courage, honesty, and compassion in a safe-deposit box. What we need is a plan—a long-term strategy to convey our convictions to the next generation.

Tim Kimmel

A good name is to be chosen rather than great riches,
Loving favor rather than silver and gold.

Proverbs 22:1

The quotes by John Luther and Tim Kimmel are quite intriguing. They both clearly state that money does not buy character. On the contrary, they shout that character is developed by the strategic investment of time over a long period. No shortcuts, no amount of money, can reverse this principle. Character development simply takes time.

However, many parents have lived their lives in a hurry, amassing plenty of financial capital only to realize too late that those they would leave the money to (their children) have no character. The truth of this principle was never more evident than in the lives of a couple Julie and I recently met.

Roger and Linda lived in a nice subdivision in an affluent section of town with their two children—a son and a daughter. Roger held a significant management position with a prestigious manufacturing firm in town, and Linda had been with a local accounting firm for the past fifteen years. She enjoyed the interaction with the other adults, and her income enabled them to enjoy the finest vacations and to frequently buy nice, new cars. She could also afford a nanny to watch the children while they were young.

The children were attractive and always had the best designer clothes and now, as teenagers, the fanciest cars. They did well in school and excelled in athletics. That is why what happened on that October night came as such a shock to Roger and Linda, as well as to the entire community.

The two children—ages eighteen and sixteen—along with two of their friends attempted to steal a new car from the local Cadillac dealership. In the chase that followed they destroyed three cars in addition to their own. All four children were injured and spent varying amounts of time in the hospital.

In this case society was affected negatively (by personal injury and destruction) because these children were lacking social capital. The parents had given them things but not the character to relate to and interact in society. Now as the children serve time in juvenile detention centers, it is too late to start the building process. Character development must begin at birth and continue into the teen years. Roger and Linda learned the hard way that the time they spent earning their money should have been balanced with more time with their children, time not only to train them but also to look for warning signs of a lack of character.

The dilemma Roger and Linda experienced is the paradox that confronts each of us: We put our best time and our best emotional energy into making money only to realize that the things that are really important (character qualities) cannot be bought with money. This is why we must balance our time and our pursuit of money.

What are some of the critical character, or social capital, building blocks needed by our posterity for them to be effective, positive, productive members of society? The list would include a work ethic, responsibility, manners, sacrifice, stewardship, teachability, accountability, loyalty, integrity, learning trade-offs, honesty, discipline, ability to interact with adults, endurance, courage, morality, and self-esteem. Although one can have good social capital without spiritual capital, it seems that the long-term motivation for social capital flows from spiritual capital, i.e., from principles.

Many good books have been written on how to train children and how to build these character qualities into them. It is not my intent to revisit the content or methods in these books. The purpose of this chapter is to look at the impact finances can have on parents' ability to inculcate these qualities into their posterity.

A Work Ethic

A work ethic is an essential component of developing character qualities into one's posterity. *Work ethic* can be defined as "the undertaking of the duty and obligation to exert physical and emotional energy in the person for a purpose." (In the next two chapters we'll look at how this purpose is likely to be different for sons and daughters.) A work ethic is understanding the need to toil or labor—*to work*—to exercise influence in an environment. A work ethic is in contrast to leisure, which is not involved in toil or labor but rather to be at ease. Laziness is adverse to labor.

Learning to work rather than being lazy is essential for at least two reasons. First, working embellishes responsibility, discipline, endurance, sacrifice, and accountability. Although these qualities may be taught without working, they cannot be taught as well. Second, since work (employment or effort that is productive and has a positive impact on society) is God's idea, children will only experience fulfillment as they learn to work. In other words, work is the alternative to slothfulness. The former will enhance a good self-image and fulfillment; the latter will destroy them.

The first step in building this component into our posterity is to teach them *God's view of work.* They must be taught to view work as good (see Genesis 2), as a gift from God (see Eccles. 5:18–19), and as an activity that God commands (see 2 Thess. 3:10). Unfortunately, the society we live in views work as a curse. That is why retirement is at the forefront of most people's thinking. The faster they can quit working, they think, the better.

Unfortunately, many of us communicate this work-is-awful thinking to our children. We complain each morning as we leave for work about having to go to work, or our children hear us complaining at dinner about how bad work is. This is why it is so important to enjoy what we do and manifest the truth of Colossians 3:23 in our lives. We must do our work heartily as though we are doing it for the Lord.

The bottom line is that you do not need to overwork to make money to quit.

A second component in teaching the work ethic is to *model it* for our children. In other words, I need to be working. This is where the tie-in with money and how one earns it becomes quite interesting. What if at age twenty-eight your financial ship came in and you inherited five million dollars? What would you do? I am sure your first thought would be to quit working. After all, that would give you a lot more time to spend with your children and train them, right? Partially. You would have more time to train them in some areas, but you cannot teach them to work if you are not working. Also, if you are not working, how would you teach them about responsibility, punctuality, discipline, "stick-to-it-iveness," perseverance, and courage? These characteristics are all part of the work-ethic package.

Why be in a big hurry to make a lot of money to quit working or buy a lot of frills (lawn service, cleaning service, a television for every room) when quitting work or buying frills could make it more difficult to train your posterity in some of these essential character areas? I do not want to imply that you cannot create an environment to teach your children some of these essential character traits if you are financially independent. However, it does appear that God, in His infinite wisdom, does accomplish a lot more through our working than if He just provided us with money. (One caution: If you do not keep balance in your work, i.e., if you constantly overwork, you will model that work is more important than family or church.)

Many years ago I met with an individual whose investment income was sufficient to meet his needs for his family without working. His children were in their early teens. When I visited him I was surprised to see him working to build his own house at the same time he was getting involved in another business. When I asked why he was going to all this effort, he explained that it was so he could train his children how to work.

The bottom line is that you do not need to overwork to make money to quit working. Likewise, overworking to have a lot of frills could make it tougher for you to build some essential character traits into your children. If you do happen to have a lot of money, you may need to act as if you don't have it, at least in the formative years of your posterity. It may be better for them to see you mowing the grass, wallpapering the house, and fixing the faucet than always seeing someone else do it just because you can afford to hire the help. This is especially true today when most of us work away from home, thus limiting the opportunity for our children to observe us working.

Finally, to teach our posterity a good work ethic, we must *let them work*. There is probably no area we have mixed up more than this one. We overwork to earn the extra money to hire a lawn service while our teenage sons play Nintendo (which we also worked hard to buy). We overwork to get a cleaning service so our daughters can go to the mall with their friends rather than help with the housework. We overwork to buy things for our younger children rather than let them work and earn the money to buy the things themselves. If we let our children work they gain a sense of accomplishment and of being part of the team. Self-image is enhanced when children do things for themselves and are productive.

It is much easier for me to take out the garbage, empty the dishwasher, set the table, run the vacuum, and feed the dog than teach my sons how to do it. I can do it faster and without any problems while the kids may break a dish or forget the dog or miss half the carpet. But how else are they going to learn? I remember the weeping and gnashing of teeth when I explained to my two oldest sons that they had certain responsibilities and chores around the house—all without financial remuneration! It was not fair, they said. When I then explained that other things could be done—clean windows or vacuum the basement—to earn various amounts of money, they immediately complained that the amount was too low. But I knew I needed to teach them to work and also teach them the value of money. If I make money too easy to come by at home, they will be in for a rude awakening in the real-world job market.

It may be easier to let my children work if I do not have a lot of money.

There is an infinite number of ways to let your children work. Those ways will change based on the different ages of your children and your specific situation. It is not so much what they do but that they begin to work and do something. It is also important that they learn to finish what they start—to stick with it and see the project through to the end.

Once again, it is interesting to note that it may be easier to let my children work if I do not have a lot of money. The issue of housecleaning or lawn mowing will be settled; the children will have to do it because I cannot afford to hire it out. I may not be as inclined to buy everything for them. They may have to sacrifice and work for some of the extra things rather than having the expectation that they will get them from me.

Individuals who have a lot of discretionary income and are, in essence, financially independent, in many cases not only retard the work ethic of their children but their affluence creates expectations in their children that may be unrealistic for them to attain later in life. The children could have a high lifestyle expectation but no work ethic to even come close to funding their expectations. This can lead to a life of disappointment.

This is not to say that money could not be used to embellish some positives in the family. As we discussed earlier, money invested to buy time at different stages of your children's lives may enhance your training opportunities. Also, extra money to buy a lake home or take nice vacations together as a family may be great. The money, however, is not essential. It could be that camping out at the lake rather than owning a lake home or a creative, inexpensive vacation rather than the expensive vacation may be more effective.

Be careful not to fall into the trap of thinking that money (and lots of it) is all that is important. It may be even more difficult to build the foundation of social capital into our children if we have a lot of money than if we don't. Consider the following comments by Randy Alcorn:

> When we mistake the giving of material things for the sharing of grace, we do a great disservice to our children. A child who grows up getting most of what he wants has a predictable future. Unless he learns to overcome his upbringing, he will misuse credit, default on his debts, and be a poor worker. He will function as an irresponsible member of his family, church, and society. He will be quick to blame others, to pout about his misfortunes, and to believe that his family, church, country, and employer—if he has one—owe him. Having counseled numerous such adults, I believe many of them are this way because their parents, sincere but misguided, led them down that very path.
>
> Parents who indulge their children out of "love" should realize that, far from loving them in the true

> sense, they are performing child abuse of the spirit and character. Though there are no laws against it—no laws of man anyway—such mistreatment will often result in more long-term personal and social damage than physical abuse.[1]

An interesting question now is, are you really better off in the scope of eternity if you are financially unable to indulge your children?

The "I-Don't-Want-My-Kids-to-Have-It-Like-I-Did" Syndrome

One of the greatest hindrances to the development of social capital in our children is the feeling that we want our children and grandchildren to "have it better" than we did. I cannot recount the number of times I have heard people say, "I just don't want my kids to go through what I went through," or "I want to give them what I didn't have."

Typically, the attitude behind these statements translates into an effort to make a lot of money to protect the children and give them things the parents did not have. "What is wrong with that?" you ask. Well, did you learn and develop the character you have by getting everything you wanted and not having to do without some things? This attitude of not wanting our kids to have it like we did often leads to overwork, and as a consequence, is devastating to the development of character qualities.

Our generation, which grew up in the thirties, forties, and fifties, had to work hard, adapt to not getting everything we wanted, and learn to wait (delayed gratification) and to understand there are trade-offs. As a result we have become the most productive generation mankind has ever seen, from a financial standpoint. Yet our generation is turning around and crippling our children and grandchildren. The very things we learned because we did not have everything we wanted we now keep our children from experiencing!

This attitude of not wanting our kids to have it like we did often leads to overwork and, as a consequence, is devastating to the development of character qualities.

In many cases, we are totally out of balance in earning money to buy all these things for our children that we did not have. So we lose on both fronts. First, we are not spending time with our posterity, and second, the things we are buying are making it more difficult (if not impossible) for them to develop the character traits they need.

When I was a junior in high school I played on the high school basketball team. That was twenty-three years ago and a time when the athletic shoe selection was not that great. As a matter of fact, until my junior year, the only basketball shoe available was the canvas Converse. That year, however, the leather Adidas with three black stripes came on the market. It was the "high-class" shoe. Everybody on the team had that shoe—except me. My parents could not afford the thirty-dollar Adidas, so I had to stick with the eight-dollar canvas shoe. Was I deprived? I thought so then. However, I learned that the shoe had nothing to do with how you played. My character was enhanced by what I did not have, and my self-image was bolstered as I was able to deal with my peers' comments about my looking different.

Earning your money with balance is the key to building social capital into your children.

I am not implying that I could not have learned these same lessons by having the Adidas shoes. I am saying that not having money may make it easier to teach our children some of the trade-offs that are important for them to develop social capital. Today I can afford to buy my boys Nike Air shoes. And it may be all right to do that. But then again, maybe it would be better not to buy them. The issue is this: They still need to learn they cannot have everything they want. Therefore, if I have a lot of money I may need to make decisions as if I do not have a lot of money. If that is the case, then it does not really matter if I have a lot of money or not. Because this is true, it does not make sense to overwork to make a lot of money to cripple my children.

I hope you get the point. If you are in a vocation that does not generate a lot of income, do not despair. It may be easier for you to build character traits into your children than if you have a lot of extra money. If you do have a lot of money, be warned that you need to be very careful how you use it. Earning your money with balance is the key to building social capital into your children.

Foundation of Values

Now, do not overreact to these comments and move into an apartment, give away the car, and starve your children so you can teach them how to be hungry and adapt to tough times! Do not make them wear old or torn clothes so they will be ridiculed and thus develop character qualities. There is a fine line between money's being a detriment instead of being a positive.

If we do not build character qualities into our children, a duty that takes time and may or may not take money, then we will continue to see a decline in our society. In a 1992 article in *World* magazine, Chuck Colson stated it this way: "The values erosion is largely responsible for the economic problems now facing the nation."[2] He illustrated this by noting that an epidemic of crime is costing billions, family breakdowns are costing billions more, and abandonment of the work ethic has meant loss of billions in productivity.

Values are foundational to any society. I hope it won't be said of us that we have deteriorated to the point that we do not focus on values at all.

For Further Reflection

1. Have you ever said you want your children to have it better than you had it? Why did you make this comment?

2. In what ways did you learn how to work as a child?

3. In what ways are you helping your children learn a work ethic? In what ways could you enhance their understanding of this concept and subsequently the character qualities of responsibility and discipline?

4. Do you agree that it is potentially more difficult to teach a work ethic and to help our children learn tradeoffs if you have money than if you do not have money?

10

A Chip Off the Old Block

The Financial Legacy We Leave to Our Sons

The almighty dollar bequeathed to a child is an almighty curse. No man has the right to handicap his son with such a burden as great wealth. He must face this question squarely: Will my fortune be safe with my boy and will my boy be safe with my fortune?

Andrew Carnegie

It is every man's duty to strive to give his children the best possible equipment for life. But to leave millions to young sons is dangerous. Each of us is better for having to make our own money in the world. . . . To take from anyone the incentive to work is a questionable service.

A. P. Giannini, head of Bank of America

Do you see a man who excels in his work?
He will stand before kings; he will not stand before unknown men.

Proverbs 22:29

One day a young man called and asked me to meet him for a private consultation at a local restaurant. When I arrived, it was not difficult to pick out the man I was to meet. Although dressed in an expensive leather jacket and a button-down oxford-cloth shirt and Gucci loafers, he was obviously ill at ease. When we shook hands I noticed his grip was somewhat limp, and he had difficulty holding eye contact. And as we made our way to a table, his conversation communicated a lack of confidence and direction as well as plenty of frustration.

I was sure this young man had either been given significant financial resources (thus, the look of affluence) through an inheritance from his or his wife's family or that he was now involved in a family business and was drawing a big income even though he was not productive in the business. I suspected this would account, in part, for his lack of self-confidence.

As the young man talked, it became apparent that my suspicions were correct. He was a third-generation player in a family business dating back to the Depression. He had received some trust funds from his grandfather when he turned twenty-one and now was in the business with his father. He was a vice president in the company, but he really did not do much for his salary, and his dad still made all the decisions.

This young man, like so many in his situation, was not "safe" with the fortune of his father and grandfather because he had not been taught how to handle the fortune, and the fortune came to him in a form (the business) that did not build on his strengths and skills. As a result, the boy's self-image and feeling of significance were sacrificed as he chafed under the burden of the fortune he was handed. He had come to me to determine if there was any business in which he could invest so he could feel good about himself.

Most fathers are building financial capital because they are convinced that is the legacy they want to leave their sons. Furthermore, they are convinced that financial capital is what their sons want and need. In this chapter we'll explore spiritual and social capital needs of our *sons* specifically, and we'll discuss briefly how financial capital in the form of a closely held business can have a negative impact on the sons' spiritual and social capital development. In the next chapter we'll address these issues as they pertain to daughters.

The Need for a Role Model

The expression seems trite, but it is true: "More is caught than taught." If the next generation of sons is to manifest the social and spiritual capital desired, they must have fathers who will model these characteristics for them. They need to see their fathers modeling a balance between work, family, church, and the community. They need their fathers to have a relationship with God, not just to be religious. They need to see a dad who works hard but still has time to play ball with them. They need to see a dad who loves their mother and is willing to talk about the business, his career, and his job with her and the family. They need to see a father who is concerned about an eternal standard of living above and beyond a current standard of living. This modeling is only possible if the dad takes time to purposefully train his sons.

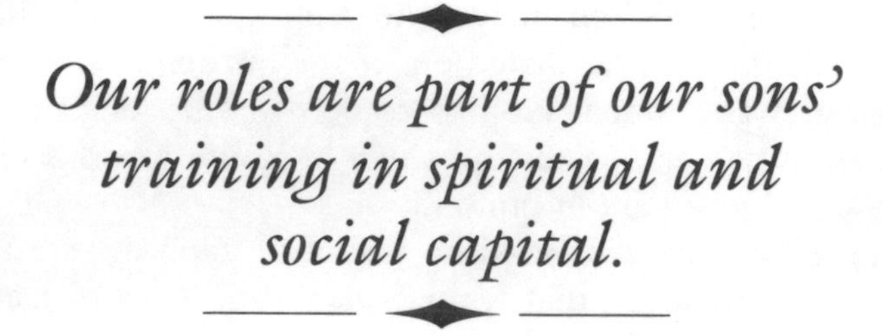

The father in this process must model for his sons *the correct role of the man in the family*—his job description, if you will. Correct roles are important to good marriages, and good marriages are the key to good families, and good families are essential to the raising up of godly descendants. Society needs men who know what their God-given roles are and who fulfill those roles. The Bible has much to say about roles, and many other books address this subject too. My goal here is to mention a few of the roles of the man in the marriage relationship as they relate to our discussion of money and family. Remember, these roles are not character qualities. A role is positional; it goes with the job. Our roles are part of our sons' training in spiritual and social capital. The key roles of a husband and father are leadership, protection, and provision.

The Key Role of Leadership

The young man picked up his date at her home and was anxious to head to the movie. The only problem was that his date was not in the car. He ran around to the driver's side and hopped in, only to realize partway down the block that his date was still standing by the street in front of her house—waiting for him to open the door for her.

This situation, though humorous, is quite revealing. We are not teaching our sons a very fundamental truth about their relationship to girls and ultimately to their wives. The Bible is clear that the man is the head of the marriage (1 Cor. 11:3). With that headship comes the responsibility for leadership, and the best leadership is servant-leadership. Thus we need to teach our sons how to be *servant-leaders.*

Though the act of opening a car door may seem old-fashioned and outdated, it helps a young man understand servant-leadership. The boy can see what "looking out for" and having the girl's best interest at heart means. The act of taking a girl's arm and helping her across the street or pulling out a chair for her accomplishes the same thing. These small actions are not necessary because the young lady is incapable of opening the door or walking across the street or sitting down on her own. Rather, they are necessary because they develop in the young man the principle of being the *leader* and the *head.*

I have three young sons, and one way I help them better understand this concept is to insist that they let their mother go through doors first. "Ladies first!" is always the cry of my five-year-old when we approach a restaurant. (We do get some funny looks as their mom walks through first.)

One of the greatest impediments to leadership in sons is the inability of some fathers to let their sons be independent and make decisions on their own. Doing everything for the son and not letting him make some mistakes or suffer failure compromises his leadership and his feelings of accomplishment and significance. To this day I feel very inadequate about working on cars. When my father fixed the cars and trucks around our farm, he basically did it himself while I held the tools. As a consequence, I did not learn how to fix anything on the car, and I feel intimidated anytime something needs to be repaired.

Many fathers do not stand aside and let sons perform some functions because it is easier for the fathers to do it themselves. The fathers know they can do it right, and they don't want to take the time to explain the process or redo it if the sons do it wrong. There it is again—the issue of time.

One of the greatest impediments to leadership in sons is the inability of some fathers to let their sons be independent and make decisions on their own.

Also tied in with the concept of leadership is the concept of self-image. As we let our sons do things on their own—make decisions, fail, and succeed—they develop a good self-image, which is a critical part of the man's ability to love his wife the way Christ loves the church (see Eph. 5:28). Helping our sons develop leadership qualities and a good self-image is an investment in their future marriage. As Abraham Lincoln said, "You cannot build character and courage by taking away man's initiative and independence. You cannot help men permanently by doing for them what they could and should do for themselves."[1]

One way to help our sons gain a sense of accomplishment is to encourage them in vocations that match their skills and abilities. If the family business does not fit that category, we should agree to convert our capital (the business) into a form that could better be used by them. Our business might be sold or a portion converted to cash to enable our son to use his subsequent inheritance to supplement his bent. If we don't convert it during our lifetime, it will be converted at death. A business left to sons who do not have the aptitude to handle it will be squandered or sold. (I'm convinced that this is the reason only 30 percent of businesses make it to the second generation and only 13 percent of businesses make it to the third generation.[2]) Too many fathers try to pass on an asset (such as the business) to children who are ill-equipped to handle it. If our sons have an aptitude for the family business we don't need to convert it, but we do need to let them contribute to the business in such a way that they feel significant.

Helping our sons develop leadership qualities and a good self-image is an investment in their future marriage.

Most fathers, however, never give their sons a chance to make their own mark in the family business because they rarely feel their sons are ready to make major business decisions. In effect, they say, "Yes, son, you're sixty years old, but you are not ready to take over." Family-business expert Leon Danco said, "It's amazing, but I had an 89-year-old businessman, still running his company, come to me to shape up his son. 'Talk to him,' he told me. The 'kid' was 57."[3] Danco recalled an evening spent with a senior vice president of a California electronics firm owned by his father. The vice president told Danco:

> There is no trust or faith in me. . . . My father treats me like I was a kid. I make a half-million dollars' worth of decisions every month, most of them the right ones, and am still second-guessed. He doesn't do that with the other executives. I'll be president, I'm sure of it because I'm qualified, but I may die or go nuts before it happens. He has promised to retire and semi-retire for the last 10 years. I've laid it on the line. One more year of this and I walk. It is a bad scene.[4]

It is my experience that men who have started businesses typically find it more difficult to let their sons make decisions and have responsibilities than do men who are employees with salary-type positions. The reason for this is that they have built something from scratch (that they've usually named after themselves—see Ps. 49:11) and they don't want anybody (including their sons) to mess it up. Their pride in what they have created makes it incredibly difficult, and in many cases impossible, to consider any alternative besides leaving it to their sons. But the sons must do things like the fathers did it. A quote from Danco put it this way: "The father kept waiting for a perfect carbon copy of himself rather than accept an imperfect original. He could not accept that there may be a different way to do some things he had been doing for thirty years. So rather than risk it by letting the son implement some new ideas he squelched it and at the same time squelched his son."[5]

One way to help our sons gain a sense of accomplishment is to encourage them into vocations that match their skills and abilities.

The non-owner (employee) typically doesn't have the same pride of craft or ownership as the founder/owner of a company, so the pressure to see a son follow in his footsteps is usually not as great. In many cases the employee could not "leave" his position to his son even if he wanted to. Consider the controller or sales manager at a large manufacturing company. Neither one has the same challenge as the founder of that company has when it comes to answering the question, "What should my son do?"

Our sons need to be allowed to follow their bents within or outside of the family business and be productive and develop into leaders. Leadership is the sought-after character trait. The business considerations are secondary.

The Key Role of Protection

The second part of a man's role is to be a *protector*. I remember vividly the frustration in Julie's voice when she explained to me how our 1977 Cutlass would haltingly enter the main road next to our home. She was sure it would die one of the times she was trying to pull onto the road and she would be broadsided! I explained to her that it was all in how she used the accelerator, but that was not the issue. She felt unprotected. Just as I had taken the steps to make sure we had adequate life insurance to protect her at my death and made sure we had locks on the doors, I needed to protect her with dependable transportation.

As I provide protection for Julie, I want my sons to understand their God-given role to protect the women in their lives. Initially, it will be their dates. They can protect them by not keeping them out too late. They can protect their dates by walking on the curbside of the sidewalk. They can protect them by offering them their coat if they get caught in unexpected cold weather.

These ideas may seem trite and you undoubtedly will have additional thoughts, but don't lose sight of the big picture here. We must teach our sons their God-given roles in the marriage relationship if they are to have strong marriages and leave a godly posterity.

The Key Role of Provision

The final part of a man's role is to *provide*. In 1 Timothy 5:8 a man who does not provide for his household is said to be worse than an unbeliever. In Genesis 3:17–19, God said man would be responsible to provide for himself and his family all the days of his life, and it would require hard work to do it.

But today's society has muddied this clear biblical principle. Young children grow up not knowing who is in charge or who is supposed to provide. This leads to rudderless families. One thing I have done since my sons were very young is to explain to them why I go to work. I want them to know that I do not just leave every day and go into some never-never land only to reappear in the evening. I want them to know that I work because God commands it and because I, not Julie, am responsible to provide for the family.

I was encouraged by the report Julie and I received after returning from a three-day trip. The couple who kept the children had evidently gotten into a discussion about work with Clark, our oldest, who was four at the time. Not expecting such a precise answer, the man asked Clark, "What does your daddy do?" Without batting an eye, Clark replied, "He is a financial planner." Slightly taken aback, the man inquired further, "What does your daddy do as a financial planner?" Clark confidently answered, "He provides for his family!"

Obviously, the best way for sons to learn to provide is to see their dad providing. This is why even if an individual is financially independent he should work in order to model a correlation between work and provision for his sons. The opposite of provision and production is consumption. Teaching our sons to be consumptive rather than productive is a significant factor. Failing to learn this distinction contributes not only to the erosion of financial capital from one generation to the next but also to the breakdown of many marriages in second and third generations.

Consumer Versus Producer

The scenario is familiar; Dad, the absentee provider, has been building his financial house. He has been a producer while at the same time he has been buying his children toys to consume. This is the natural response to his not spending time with his children. Rather than give them his time or teach them to work, he indulges them with material things to consume. Perhaps without even being aware of it, he develops in them a consumption mentality rather than a production mentality. The children come to expect the toys and the trappings their dad's wealth can buy them. The resulting patterns are predictable.

For the son who has learned to be consumptive rather than productive, an interesting dilemma could result. As he attempts to follow his vocational interests—getting a job that maximizes his skills and strengths in the marketplace—he cannot generate enough income to support the lifestyle to which he has become accustomed. If his dad's wealth is not in the form of a closely held business, the son's only alternative is to get a job that will support his lifestyle. This usually results in his seeking the highest-paying jobs regardless of whether he is equipped for those jobs. So begins a frustrating life of moving from one job to another trying to support his consumptive need, or of being in a job he does not enjoy just for the income it provides.

If a son cannot find a job to support his lifestyle, he may continue to look to his dad for handouts, which keeps him dependent on his dad. This can be an unhealthy situation, not only for the son, but also for his marriage. (We'll discuss this in more detail later in this chapter.)

This consumption mentality and dependence are most common in the closely held family business because this business usually affords the founder and his family significant income and the corresponding perks that come with that income. Also, the son has usually worked there while growing up, and he is expected to come into the business after finishing high school or college. As a result, a son may try another line of work because of his interests but if he finds that kind of work cannot support his consumptive lifestyle, he easily returns to the family business. Although a consumption mentality is usually the reason for a son's migrating back to the family business, it is not the only reason. In some cases, the son's fear of disappointing his dad is so great (especially in "only" sons) that he will go back to the business even though it is not really what he wants to do.

So why does a dad let his son come into the business and draw out a handsome salary even though he knows the son is not productive or fulfilled? Dad likes having him there because down deep he has convinced himself that he can leave the business to his son, and his financial legacy will live on after he is gone. This is not what happens, however.

A son who is in his dad's business because of the money he needs and not because he contributes to the business can be caught in a dangerous trap. The other employees know the son is not productive enough to warrant the income he is making, and the son knows it too. He has no feeling of accomplishment or significance, so he finds a cause that needs him or he does dangerous and outlandish things; he goes on safaris, races cars or sailboats, or conquers the Boston

Marathon. He spends his entire life trying to find himself.

Danco's experience confirms mine. He stated:

> The business owners' sons are usually oversold and underdeveloped. . . . The problem is that so many [sons] don't get the chance [to do anything productive in the business] so they become embittered and emasculated. They end up being non-economic beings—playboys, dilettantes, or just bums.[6]

Even more devastating is the son who has been trained to be consumptive and who does not have the business to fall back on to support his consumption because the family business has been sold. In many cases, he may have gotten a lump sum from the sale, but that principal is dissipated rapidly. Only when the son runs totally out of money does he even try to be productive, but then he can't because he does not know how. This typically leads to a life of drifting from one job to the next and barely making it.

A son who is in his dad's business because of the money he needs and not because he contributes to the business can be caught in a dangerous trap.

A son who is dependent on the business or handouts from his dad to support his habit of consumption is not unlike a person on drugs. He is just as dependent and just as trapped. He has a habit he cannot break, and that habit can devastate him personally and in his marriage. A contributing factor to many divorces is the inability of the husband (the son in our present discussion) to sever ties to his father.

Many families in America have generated significant fortunes only to see them lost because they trained their children to consume rather than to produce. Is it any wonder the saying "shirtsleeves to shirtsleeves in three generations" is accurate? Why not teach sons to be productive and be in shirtsleeves in each generation? If a son is taught to be productive and not consumptive, then whatever he earns vocationally will probably support his lifestyle. He will be free to pursue a vocation that fits his skills and abilities.

A trust fund that has significant assets in it can have the same effect on a son as a business. In many cases the son tends to be consumptive and waits for the trust to be distributed. I know of a young man who spent the first twenty years of his adult life scuba diving and riding motocross in the summer and skiing here and in Europe in the winter. He has not lived a productive day in his adult life; he just expects the trust to provide for him. Unfortunately, the assets are significant enough that they will probably last his lifetime, but his children are in for a rude awakening. They will have to be productive because there will be no money for them.

No father would want to see his son become dependent on drugs. Yet by making him a consumer and dependent on a family-owned business or a trust fund, he does almost as great a disservice. He runs the risk of undermining his son's self-image and his son's marriage and of limiting his own ability to ever transfer assets to that son.

If a son is taught to be productive and not consumptive, then whatever he earns vocationally will probably support his lifestyle. He will be free to pursue a vocation that fits his skills and abilities.

This concept of consumption versus production and its corresponding problems is highlighted in Patrick Reynolds's book, *The Gilded Leaf*. Patrick, the grandson of R. J. Reynolds of the Reynolds tobacco family, described his grandfather as a canny politician, a workaholic, and a farsighted risk-taker who built the business. According to Patrick, two of R. J.'s sons, Dick and Smith, became irresponsible playboys. After four failed marriages, Patrick Reynolds wrote, Dick Reynolds died "a troubled recluse," leaving a confusing will that threw his family into chaos. About himself, Patrick wrote:

> I was raised with the Reynolds name—but not the family.

> I knew that at 21 I would inherit $2.5 million—a legacy from my grandmother. That was a mixed blessing.
>
> I developed an interest in filmmaking. But rather than work my way up in a production company, learning to be part of a group, I attended film festivals and classes, and spent hours in my expensive film-editing laboratory—always alone. At first, my inherited wealth isolated me since I didn't need to get a job, depend on others, etc. Later, when I wanted work as an actor, the fact that I didn't need to work was held against me.
>
> I enjoyed a youthful period of Hollywood high-life. Then, seeking stability, I married . . . and subsequently, as had become the fashion, I divorced, too.
>
> I thought I could outdo my father and grandfather, and achieve a massive fortune. But, untutored in the world of business, I made a series of bad investments. That erosion of capital finally forced me to join society.[7]

Patrick Reynolds's advice in his book is consistent with my theory of posterity: "provide your children with plenty of personal guidance. Spend time with them. Boarding schools cannot take the place of effective parenting. Require that they live on money that they earn well into their 20s—or even their 30s. Reason: This allows them to establish a firm identity and sense of self-worth."[8]

Four Critical Needs of Our Sons

Our sons have four critical needs to develop sound social and spiritual capital. First, we fathers need to make sure our sons feel the freedom to do whatever God equips and calls them to do. They may have different goals, dreams, and aspirations than we do, and they should be allowed to pursue these dreams and desires. A son pursuing a different vocation is not in any way a suggestion that what his father has done for years is of no value or significance. It is just an acknowledgment that God has made each person different. Let's tell them we will not be disappointed if they do not follow us into our business.

Second, if our sons do come into the business with us after they are married, we need to realize our relationship with them is now different from when they were single. I know of several marriages that became rocky because the father continued to make the same requests of his son (now the husband) that he always had—to work late, to go on family vacations with the parents, to join him on hunting trips, and so on. These types of requests can put the son in an awkward position—having to decide between disappointing the father by saying no (which he never did before) or frustrating his wife by saying yes. A wise dad will be careful not to put his son in these kinds of positions.

Third, if sons follow in their fathers' steps vocationally, they need to be allowed to make their own mark on the business. Today's sons have grown up in a different era with different training and education. As a result, they will have different ideas about how things should be done in the business and when they should be done. They need to be allowed to implement their ideas (or at least some of them) so they can establish an identity and a feeling of significance. Just because something has been done a certain way for thirty years does not mean it is the right way to do it today. In this computer age of increasing knowledge, evolving technology, and expanding information networks, experience is not what it used to be. New ideas and innovations come quickly, and our sons may know more about those changes than we do.

Finally, we need to let our sons struggle to find their own way. If a butterfly is helped out of its cocoon and not allowed to struggle out, it will die. The struggling strengthens the butterfly so it can fly. Similarly, we should be careful not to use our money to "help" our sons or allow our money to make it too easy for them so that they are crippled for life. Like the butterfly, they must be allowed to fly their own path and chart their own course. Although it's sometimes hard to do, we must be able to let them go.

Although sons will undoubtedly be different from us, they will still be chips off the old block. The key for fathers, however, is that they be a chip of the same social and spiritual values as the Father.

Sons need fathers who love them enough to let them find their way while the father still serves as their guide, their mentor, their model. Sons need fathers who allow them to be different yet love them unconditionally. Sons need fathers who are as concerned about their social and spiritual growth as they are about the growth of the sons' careers. Sons need fathers who take seriously the charge in Ephesians 6:4, "Fathers, do not provoke your children to wrath, but bring them up in the training and admonition of the Lord."

I find it interesting that this passage is addressed to fathers but not to mothers. This implies that we, as fathers, have the tendency to exasperate our children. The ideas discussed in this chapter are one area where we could create this exasperation. We need to ask God for wisdom and strength so this won't be the case.

For Further Reflection

1. Discuss some ways you are teaching your son to lead.

2. Have you found that your son has been different from you? If so, in what ways has he been different?

3. Have you found these differences hard to deal with?

4. How are you teaching your son to protect and provide?

5. If you have a closely held business, has this chapter challenged your thinking? If so, in what way?

11

DADDY'S LITTLE GIRL

THE FINANCIAL LEGACY WE LEAVE TO OUR DAUGHTERS

Then we put on our suits and ties, packed our brief-cases and took off on this Great Experiment, convinced that there was no difference between ourselves and the guys in the other offices. How wrong we were. Because like it or not, women have babies. It's this biological thing that's just there, these organs we're born with. The truth is, a woman can't live the true feminist life unless she denies her childbearing biology.

Kay Ebeling, *Newsweek*

Every wise woman builds her house,
But the foolish pulls it down with her hands.

Proverbs 14:1

Julie and I work in the four-year-old class at church on Sunday mornings. It is always amazing to observe the children and their differences, especially between the boys and the girls. When the girls come in they typically sit down to color (staying in the lines, I might add) or sing songs with one of the teachers. Not the boys. They are usually wrestling on the floor or throwing something. If they do sit down to color, the paper is vigorously covered with scribbles on both sides; after all, why should one be constrained by the lines?

God created male and female equally, but He definitely designed them as distinct and unique creations, as Genesis 1:27 tells us: "God created man in His own image; in the image of God He created him; *male* and *female* He created them" (emphasis added). We live in a society, however, that tells us that there is really no difference (which makes me believe society must not have observed a four-year-old class or, for that matter, observed their own sons and daughters very carefully). As the differences between male and female have become more and more muted, so too has the issue of money and our daughters. Should we involve our daughters in the family business? Should they be treated the same way we treat our sons? What are their spiritual and social capital needs, and how do we use our money to enhance the development of those needs? What is their greatest need from their fathers? In this chapter we will look for answers to these questions, examining the impact our money (and how we use it and leave it) can have on our daughters.

Daddy's Little Girl and the Business

As we have already discussed, many fathers have a built-in desire to bring their children into the family business. Implementing this desire, though complex when sons are involved, can be even more complicated when daughters are involved.

The first complication has to do with the emotional differences between a son and a daughter. David M. Marson, president of Newcan, a manufacturer of metal tubes and components for the filter industry, made this clear in an interview with *Family Business* magazine. He stated:

> Would the transition (of the business) have been easier if Marsha had been a man? Frankly, yes. There would have been fewer barriers to break down, fewer precedents to establish. It would have been easier for me, and I would not have had as many concerns about the present and the future. I suppose I feel that I could commit a son to long hours, hard work, and the uncertainty of the future without the same worries as with a daughter. Those concerns were based not on doubts about her ability, but on emotional elements between fathers and daughters.[1]

No matter how hard fathers try to deny it or work around it, daughters have babies and different family responsibilities than sons.

Ernie Kasper, of the Kasper Foundry Co., a third-generation family business in Elyria, Ohio, said this about his daughter, Betsy, who is in the business:

> No father would ask a son how he plans to juggle the responsibilities of business and family. But when it comes to daughters, fathers do ask. The question is not daycare, or who will do the grocery shopping, or who will look after things during the three months after the baby is born. The real question is the amount of emotional energy that is extracted from

the daughter on the job that is unavailable to her own family—the founder's grandchildren.[2]

Roland Bacci, whose thirty-one-year-old daughter, Robin, took over his Mercedes-Benz dealership, had this to say: "She's so warm and so wonderful—I'd love to see her married and having children . . . that would make me happiest." But as Robin says, "The business takes all my energy, my love, and my attention." That, in a sentence, sums up why Roland is frustrated and concerned. Even though his daughter is running the business he would be happier if she were married and having his grandchildren.[3]

Daughters are different emotionally from our sons, and income and assets can affect them and their marriages differently.

A second challenge is the delicate balance of grooming the daughter to take over the business while at the same time encouraging her to be ready to step into the role of wife when she marries. To become president will require her to take on characteristics of independence, aggressiveness, and assertiveness that could go against the grain of learning the scriptural role of a wife. The Bible is clear that the wife's role includes a quiet and gentle spirit, as well as an attitude of fitting in with her husband's plans (Proverbs 31). Helping our daughters understand their biblical role (that is, developing their spiritual capital) and then encouraging them to live it out in society (developing social capital) is a critical part of the training process.

A third challenge has to do with the salary that comes with the president's office. Although most would say, "There is nothing wrong with a daughter making as much money as she can," it does create some interesting dynamics in her marriage. George Gilder's comments, in his book *Men and Marriage*, point this out. He wrote, "A woman's financial superiority may reduce the likelihood of marriage—or diminish its duration. . . . It will tend to demoralize and estrange the men around her."[4] He goes on to say, "Most men are not happy when their wives earn more than they do. When roles are reversed, with men doing the housework and women providing the income, couples become dreadfully unhappy."[5]

From these insights we can conclude that the differences between our sons and daughters should not be ignored. Daughters are different emotionally from our sons, and income and assets can affect them and their marriages differently. If most fathers are honest they will admit, as Roland Bacci did, that they really want their daughters to fulfill their God-given role as a wife and mother. If this is the case, should we not be more concerned about grooming our daughters for that role than for the role of president of the family business? Let us consider how the manner and amount of money we give to our daughters can either enhance or tear down their potential for fulfilling their God-given roles (spiritual capital) and having harmonious marriages (social capital).

Your Daughter, Her Husband, and Your Money

The Bible describes two key attitudes of a wife in a marriage relationship: submission (fitting in with her husband's plans) and respect (see Ephesians 5). It is equally clear that the man is to provide and be the head of the family (see 1 Cor. 11:3 and 1 Tim. 5:8). Since the man must feel he is the head and provider, what happens when the wife is given a large sum of money so his effort to provide for her is not needed? Obviously, his impetus to take risks and struggle to find his niche (all part of providing) will likely be thwarted. As a result, he could futilely try to find some significance while spending his days idly wasting time or doing something other than providing. This, of course, can infuriate his wife because it is her "daddy's money" they're spending while the husband is trying to find himself. She will probably let him know that, and her words can damage his feelings of self-esteem and significance even more.

What can happen to the daughter? If she is given a large sum of money either outright or through inheritance early in her marriage, she may adopt a "this is my money and I can spend it however I want" attitude. Or her attitude can insist, "I don't need to fit in with your plans, your budget, or your money." Either way, she could become independent and less apt to look to her husband to provide.

In this situation the marriage is at risk. The husband could conclude that she does not need him, and in this frame of mind he might look for someone else who really does need him. The wife could develop a feeling of superiority and independence that could cause her to decide to go it alone. Even if she does not go that far, the fact that she has all this money can put tremendous pressure on her husband to prove that he is worthy of her respect.

This was illustrated very clearly to me by a young lady who was to be the recipient of significant trust funds when she turned twenty-one. She was three months shy of that age—and eight months away from getting married—when she called our office in fear that the money would do to her marriage what she had seen it do to her mother's and grandmother's. She was wise to seek counsel, but how much wiser for parents and grandparents not to put their daughters and granddaughters in such a position in the first place.

Current gifts, if given at all, should be small, in cash, and given to both the wife and her husband.

As with sons, tremendous care should be taken by parents to think through any significant gifts they give to their married daughters. As a guideline, parents should resist making gifts of expensive cars, furniture, elite vacation homes, or nice jewelry. In short, avoid anything that could tend to make the daughter's husband feel inferior or embarrassed because he cannot provide it. Neither should gifts be made to pay for something the husband should be providing—food, utilities, or shelter. I recommend that current gifts, if given at all, should be small, in cash, and given to *both* the wife and her husband. Together they can decide what to do with the money because it is theirs, not just hers.

There is another time to give married daughters assets and larger sums of money. Once the daughter's husband has taken the provision responsibility and made a place for himself—has shown responsibility and commitment for the spiritual, social, and financial well-being of his wife and family—then the money will likely not upset the equilibrium. Regardless of the size of the gift and the timing, however, it is still best to make the gift to both the husband and the wife, not just to the daughter.

Your Daughter and Her Vocation

Most couples see nothing wrong with encouraging their daughters to get a good education and be successful in their chosen field of employment. On the surface this sounds fine, but the daughter must be encouraged to take care to fit her position in the secular world with God's job description for her in a future marriage. The issue is preparation for a godly, harmonious marriage, and in many cases the farther up the vocational ladder a woman climbs, the more difficulties she faces in her marriage.

Consider the women of Hollywood fame and glitter. How many of those who have enjoyed incredible financial success were able to stay happily married to their first husband? George Gilder's comment from *Men and Marriage* captures the problem: "Husbands often resent ambitious wives. Women themselves are found to be happier and relationships more stable when the male partners are more ambitious and successful than they."[6]

There is also a direct correlation between the amount of time and effort put into training for a vocation and the subsequent difficulty in quitting that job when children come along.

According to Gary S. Becker, an economist at the University of Chicago, "The propensity to split rises when women are doing better [financially]."[7]

Another illustration is my own marriage. I was a coach and a teacher at the local high school when I first met Julie. She was already a registered nurse, specializing as an anesthetist at Kansas University Medical Center. During our first year of marriage we both worked, as most young couples do. I soon realized, though, that Julie made more than I did and worked shorter hours. Not only did that begin to nag at me a little, but I also did not like what the job did to her attitude.

To be a successful anesthetist required adopting a take-charge mind-set, and many times this mind-set found its way home. I wanted to fulfill my role as leader, but it was difficult for Julie—who had been in charge all day—to fit into my leadership when she got home. In addition, the job demanded so much from her emotionally and physically that she had very little energy left to meet my needs when I got home.

There is also a direct correlation between the amount of time and effort put into training for a vocation and the subsequent difficulty in quitting that job when children come along. Had Julie trained to be a doctor she would have had a more difficult time quitting than she had as a nurse-anesthetist. Also, because she had specialized as a nurse-anesthetist, she had a harder time than if she had not specialized. Not only is the training time a factor, but also the amount of income earned can affect this decision. The more a woman makes, the harder it is for her to quit and train the children when they come along.

Julie's case illustrates how we can best encourage our daughters. Julie's father encouraged her to get a degree and become a nurse so she could provide for her financial needs if she never married. He also encouraged her to step out of her career when the time came to raise her children, so she would have more time to build spiritual and social capital into his future posterity.

This advice works in many situations. As a parent you should sit down with your daughter and study what God's Word says about marriage. Then help her discover what career best uses her skills and abilities so she can support herself while single without jeopardizing her future marriage. Since you do not know what God plans for her, you should ask some difficult questions. If her husband is a construction worker and she is a surgeon, will that cause conflict? If he is a pastor and she is an airline pilot, could that undermine their marriage? God says that in marriage the man is to be the head, the leader. Will her career path—perhaps even taking over your business—help or hinder her marriage relationship? These difficult questions must be examined as parents teach God's order and promote correct roles in marriage (to our daughters *and* sons).

Dads especially need to set their daughters free from their expectations in the work arena and encourage them in biblical roles. The father should encourage his daughter toward vocations that are easier to relinquish so she can fit in with her husband's plans and nurture her children.

Dads especially need to set their daughters free from their expectations in the work arena and encourage them in biblical roles.

Julie's dad seemed to understand this when he wrote her this letter after she quit work as a nurse-anesthetist:

> Now then—work. I have some thoughts to submit for your perusal. Namely—I think it is very good for you *not* to work! In my opinion you were right on to go ahead and get the training and do the job—and you did it extremely well. [Dad was an anesthesiologist, and Julie worked for his group.] But now, you are married. That changes things. The anesthesia thing is *completely* separate from Russ—and you spend *most* of your waking life in it. Whereas, by not working you spend most of your time being *wife* and involved in Russ's life. That's much better! Further, a nurse anesthetist *must* be a *strong, independent, stand-up-to-the-men* type person. . . . Those are not exactly qualities to be developed in marriage. Anyway, it just this week dawned on me that I hope you *don't* go back to it. How about that! Rather,

> you can be full-time wife and homemaker—which is a *real* and godly calling, and very, *very* wonderful. You will have plenty to do—with being available to people and to Russ.[8]

Fathers should give this gift to their daughters when they are married, freeing them from feeling they disappoint their dads if they do not make names for themselves in secular business or come back into their dads' businesses.

One caution to fathers: Be careful not to let your pride influence your counsel to your daughters. A few fathers would far rather announce that their daughter is a doctor than a nurse. Or that their daughter is going to take over the business and keep it going after they are gone. Or that their daughter just received her doctorate from a prestigious university. They seem to prefer anything rather than saying, "My daughter stays home with the children." In God's economy, however, your married daughters are more successful if they have harmonious marriages and godly children than if they have successfully taken over your business or have a significant position in the corporate world. Do not lose sight of that truth as you encourage and advise them on their vocational choices.

Consumption Versus Contentment

Just as it is with our sons, the consequences are tremendous if we teach or allow our daughters to become consumptive. For sons, the contrast was production versus consumption; for daughters, the contrast is contentment versus consumption. Of course this does not mean that our sons do not need to learn contentment; they need to learn to be content while living within their income. But the daughter does not have the responsibility of providing for the family, so the best way she can help the family is to learn to be content. From a biblical perspective, contentment is the ability to be satisfied with wherever God leads us. This can only come from maturing spiritually as we know God better.

If we give our daughters everything they want materially as they grow up, we do a tremendous disservice to their future husbands. We allow them to go into marriage with a consumption mentality, which can have dramatic consequences on their marriage.

If we give our daughters everything they want materially as they grow up, we do a tremendous disservice to their future husbands.

First, a consumption mentality sets them up for frustration when their expectations are not met by their husbands. Although they should not expect their husbands, who are just starting their careers, to have as much income as their dads (who worked for twenty-five years), most have a hard time adjusting to this. As a result, they may put pressure on their husbands to earn more and more. If the husband cannot provide enough, the wife may look to her dad for more money (much as the son did) to get the things she wants. By looking back to her dad rather than to her husband, a wife can affect the husband's self-image and feeling of significance. She remains dependent on her dad, and that dependency can be just as devastating to her personally and to her marriage as if she were dependent on drugs.

Second, if the daughter expects a certain lifestyle depicted by certain material things, she could become discontent when those things are not provided. This discontentment can have several negative consequences. Her husband may overwork in his attempt to make more money to allow her to continue to have what she wants; but as he spends more and more time at work, he has less and less time for her and the children—which can have an impact on the marriage and the raising of a godly posterity. Or he may just give up and tell her to go ahead and charge the things she wants on a credit card. Then, as the debt mounts, the pressure on him gets greater, and the cycle continues. Or he may insist that the wife go back to work. After all, he reasons, if she wants all these things she can earn the money to get them. The negative impact of the wife's working is well documented on both the marriage and the children.

Maria Monet, CEO of Ogden Corporation, has no children. She said, "I used to think I could work and raise a family. I realize now it's hard just to do my job well."[9] Phyllis Swersky, the executive vice president of AICorp Inc. states, "I am frequently too tired to tell my husband about my day, listen to him tell me about his, or play with the children. It was a major challenge just to figure out a simple hairstyle and makeup for myself. I don't cook. I don't take my children to malls and museums, and I don't have any close friends."[10]

The truth of Proverbs 14:1 stands. A wife can build up her home by being content and learning to live at the income level of her husband while a foolish woman can tear down her house by being discontent, spending consumptively, and living beyond her husband's means.

I have always appreciated Julie's attitude of contentment. She tells me she is happy with me and it does not matter what I earn. She has told me she would be happy in a tent in Alaska and that we are wealthy because we have each other. She never puts me under pressure to earn more money or buy her more things. Her life exemplifies the principle of Proverbs 31:12: "She does him good and not evil / All the days of her life."

I am convinced she is this way to a large degree because of her dad's encouragement vocationally and because both her parents modeled a frugal lifestyle. Although her dad was a doctor and they could afford anything they wanted (and they did have some nice things, including an airplane and a boat), they made it clear to Julie that these things were for the whole family to enjoy; she should not expect to continue to have them when she left home. They shopped at middle-of-the-road stores, and the children did not have to have the fanciest clothes, cars, and toys. Julie's parents modeled a heart of giving, which goes a long way toward slaying the consumptive mind-set. They taught Julie to be thankful for what she had. To this day when she feels discontented, Julie will make a list of all she has to be thankful to God for, and this helps her get her thinking back on the Lord.

Daughters *are* different from our sons, and we need to be wise in how we use our money related to them. Marriages and future generations of our posterity may depend on how well we help our daughters understand their God-given roles and develop the qualities necessary to fulfill those roles.

For Further Reflection

1. Has your wife ever earned more income than you? How did you feel about that (frustrated, intimidated, anxious, glad, maybe even insecure)?

2. Do you agree with the thoughts expressed in this chapter about how fathers should counsel their daughters vocationally? Is this realistic in today's society?

3. Do you think a daughter should take over her father's business? Why or why not?

4. What are you doing to encourage your daughter to be content and live frugally?

5. How much have you accepted the world's view of women in the workplace?

12

The Hand That Rocks the Cradle

A Man's Investment in His Wife

The highest happiness on earth is in marriage. Every man who is happily married is a successful man even if he has failed in everything else.

William Lyon Phelps

The future destiny of a child is the work of a mother.

Napoleon Bonaparte

House and riches are an inheritance from fathers,
But a prudent wife is from the LORD.

Proverbs 19:14

He who finds a wife finds a good thing,
And obtains favor from the LORD.

Proverbs 18:22

Men, husbands, dads . . . this chapter is for you. If you are like me, you have probably had a time in your marriage where your wife went to a meeting or was gone for a day or two and you had to do it all. You had to play "Mr. Mom." And like me, you probably thought it would be no problem. You could handle it with no sweat, right?

That was what I thought when Julie had to attend a funeral out of town and needed to be gone for two days. I uttered the infamous lines, "No problem. Don't worry. I can handle it." Well, I did handle the forty-eight hours, but just barely. I was able to get the kids to school, get them fed, and even get a little work done at the office. But that was it. I did not do any laundry, grocery shopping, or any of the other activities Julie does during the day to make our household run smoothly. I did not help much with homework, or sit and read to the children, or spend much time at all listening to them and answering their questions as she does. I did not have a lot of time to strategically train and pour values into them as Julie does, which, as we have seen, is so important.

Needless to say, after those forty-eight hours I had a renewed appreciation for the importance of teamwork in the whole area of posterity development! That is why our marriages are so important.

It is important in this section on how to use our money to look at the role marriage plays, not only in the development of a godly posterity, but also in the accumulation of financial capital. It's also important to look at how we can use our money to enhance our marriage and maximize training time.

The best thing we can do for our children is keep our marriages together and model for them Christ and the church. Harmonious marriages give our children a healthy and secure environment in which they can grow to be productive and godly members of society.

Posterity Implications

We have spent a lot of time looking at the importance of balancing work and family in order to have time to invest in our posterity. However, one of the best ways to invest time in our children is to invest time in developing and maintaining a harmonious marriage. Why? Because the best thing we can do for our children is keep our marriages together and model for them Christ and the church (see Ephesians 5). Harmonious marriages give our children a healthy and secure environment in which they can grow to be productive and godly members of society. I like what Dorothy Patterson, in the book *Recovering Biblical Manhood and Womanhood*, said about the divine assignment of homemaking:

> The home was once described as "a place apart, a walled garden, in which certain virtues too easily crushed by modern life could be preserved," and the mother in this home was described as "The Angel in the House." Few women realize what great service they are doing for mankind and for the kingdom of Christ when they provide a shelter for the family and good mothering—the foundation on which all else is built. A mother builds something far more magnificent than any cathedral—the dwelling place for an immortal soul (both her child's fleshly tabernacle and his earthly abode). No professional pursuit so uniquely combines the most menial tasks with the most meaningful opportunities. . . .
>
> The result of really competent mothering will be passed from generation to generation. Products in the marketplace may come and go, but generation after generation we produce our sons and daughters. A child needs his mother to be all there; to be focused on him, to recognize his problems and needs; to support, guide, see, listen to him, love and want him.[1]

Yes, motherhood is indeed a high calling and a time-consuming and demanding job. That's why I believe if we are to build the appropriate foundations of spiritual and social capital into our children, moms must get back into the home.

Obviously, the question about the single parent could come up here. What about their posterity? God's grace is sufficient in those situations to mature the children. It appears that it is much easier, however, to build the foundation of spiritual and social capital when husband and wife work together as a team. Thus there is a heightened need to develop and maintain harmony in the marriage. We need to keep it together so our posterity does not end up a part of the statistics of "children in households headed by a single parent due to divorce."

Let's look now at two ways we can use our money to get our wives back in the home and encourage them while they are there.

1. Live on the Husband's Income

We need to manage our finances in such a way that our wives do not have to work outside the home in vocational employment, especially during the children's early, formative years. Ensuring that their foundation is built securely takes time and attention. And although it is important for the father to maximize his time with the children, due to his added responsibility of earning a living for the family, it falls to the mother to provide the bulk of this building time.

We need to manage our finances in such a way that our wives do not have to work outside the home in vocational employment, especially during the children's early, formative years.

Mothers are the ones who are typically there when the children get home from school; she's the one who listens while the children enjoy a snack and talk about their day. Mothers are the ones who fix a band uniform before the big game or pick up a sick child from school. They are the ones who give the child a hug before he or she boards the school bus in the morning.

Mothers are the ones who help children get along, learn to share, be responsible, and show kindness toward others. They are the ones who need to be there at those strategic, teachable moments that occur in a child's life that are not scheduled but that define the child's future values and character. Philippa Maister, a freelance writer for the *Atlanta Journal and Constitution*, wrote, "It is this thereness that gives children self-esteem and self-confidence, security born of knowing they are the center of someone's universe, a sense of unlimited trust."[2]

This is surely why Napoleon Bonaparte made his famous statement that a child's destiny is "the work of a mother." A mother is "a wise, loving caregiver, guarding and guiding her children on the uneven road through life."[3]

Yet even though the mother has the most time with the children, the father is still the one responsible before God for the family. The story of Eli in 2 Samuel 2 illustrates this point when it records how God talked with Eli about Eli's sons. God did not talk to Eli's wife—the mother of the boys. This shows why it is essential for me to support and encourage Julie in her roles of homemaker and nurturer. To a large degree she holds in her hands the ultimate mark I will leave on society. That is why it is a joint effort and why we must manage our money in such a way that she does not need to work outside the home.

The importance of the mother's role in the posterity was also illustrated at a family reunion of G. Campbell Morgan, a great preacher whose four sons also became ministers. One of the sons was asked by a friend, "Which Morgan is the greatest preacher?" The son, while looking at his famous father, replied, "Mother!"[4]

I know many of you are thinking it would be great if your wife (or you, as a mother) could stay home, but in today's economy you just do not see how you can do it. You *need* both incomes to make it. In my book *Money and Your Marriage*, I devoted an entire chapter to the myth of the working mother. In summary, that chapter points out that, at best, a second income only contributes 50 percent of the gross income to a family's net, spendable income. And in most cases with child care and other added expenses, at least twenty thousand dollars of the mother's income is needed before any noticeable contribution is made to the family's spendable income. In other words, if she is not making more than twenty thousand dollars, she is not helping the family's financial situation at all!

In our business, we have frequent occasions to help couples work out a plan to make it on one income. We tell them the key is becoming convinced that your posterity is worth the sacrifice and then making the correct financial decisions to enable the mother to stay at home. Dads, may I be honest with you? This conviction must be *yours*. You are the God-ordained leader of the home. It is important for you to take the leadership and develop a plan so your wife can stay at home to train the only mark of importance you will ever leave on future generations.

The Governor on the Accelerator of the Home

One of the benefits (and one of the most *critical* benefits, it seems) of living on one income is the ability to slow the pace somewhat. Life is fast enough with the husband working outside the home. If the wife works outside the home also, the acceleration increases. Julie and I have found on the days she has an early meeting at school or a meeting at night, everything speeds up and tends to get out of control. We rush through breakfast or fly through dinner, barely acknowledging the children or each other. If we were both working outside the home, it would be like that twenty-four hours a day.

It is important for you to take the leadership and develop a plan so your wife can stay at home to train the only mark of importance you will ever leave on future generations.

I am convinced that the mother is the *governor on the accelerator of the home.* Her relaxed presence during the morning rush to get Dad to work and the kids to school makes it easier to have a family devotion. Her availability enables everyone to have a good breakfast rather than just a piece of toast or a donut as we fly out of the kitchen to the school bus or office. Her being there and not needing to rush to work gives her the emotional energy to help the children with homework, reading, training in good manners, citizenship, and respect. One mother observed, "At my daughter's elementary school, I've watched as exhausted women, having placed their children on the school bus at 7:00 A.M. or earlier, arrive to fetch them as late as 6:30 P.M. too tired for a hug or even a smile."[5]

For the two-income family, weekends can be just as hectic as weekdays because that's when they must catch up on errands and other chores they had to postpone during the work week. When the weekend becomes crowded, one of the first things to go is the family's Sunday-morning church attendance. As we discussed earlier, it is important for our families to attend church together (see Heb. 10:24–25) as part of the development of spiritual capital. What a travesty when the pace of our lives crowds out the Sabbath day of fellowship with God's people and rest for ourselves.

2. Understand Our Wives

It is not enough to just free our wives financially so they can stay at home; we must also invest in them spiritually and emotionally. We must apply the instruction of 1 Peter 3:7, which says, "Likewise you husbands, dwell with [your wives] with understanding, giving honor to the wife, as to the weaker vessel, and as being heirs together of the grace of life, that your prayers may not be hindered."

We need to be students of our wives and understand that they are different from us. Many good books discuss these differences: *Rocking the Roles* by Robert Lewis and *If Only He Knew* and *For Better or For Best* by Gary Smalley. Also, *Money and Your Marriage* touches on these issues as well. I will only comment here on how we can use our money to promote the spiritual and emotional well-being of our wives. I think it is important to talk of this use of money as an investment. Most men will invest their money in real estate, the stock market, and their business; yet they neglect to use some of their money to enhance their marriages.

There are several ways to make this investment. One way, as we have seen, is to be willing to make less money and buy more time to spend with our wives. Replace work time with posterity time. Remember the principle of replacement? Our wives need emotional oneness with us, and it does not really matter, in many cases, what we do during that time as long as we do it with them. When I get very busy at work and have several late nights in succession when I am late for dinner (or miss it entirely), Julie can become really frustrated. When that happens we do not have a chance to catch up on our days and talk about the children and think through our schedules; not being able to talk together reduces our oneness. By not working the extra hours and potentially making less money, I invest in my relationship with my wife.

Our wives also have a need for our spiritual leadership, so we need time to pray with them. We need time to study the Bible together and enjoy the fellowship of other believers as a couple. The only way we men can provide this leadership is if we buy time to spend with God ourselves so we have something to share with our wives. We need to balance work so we do not neglect our daily quiet time, our time of prayer with God. Why don't you ask your wife right now whether she would rather you make an additional investment in the stock market or invest some more time in a Bible study? I think I know what she will say.

The mother is the governor on the accelerator of the home.

Another way to invest in your wife is to actually spend some money to free her time. By having the latest appliances (microwaves, food processors, dishwashers, good vacuum cleaners, and efficient washers and dryers) we are able to maximize the time our wives have to spend with the children. At some times of year (especially around the holiday season), I find if I spend some money for a cleaning service for a few weeks, Julie's emotional well-being is affected in a positive way, not to mention her physical health. A timely meal out also can help her emotionally. Perhaps many mothers go to work outside the home, not because they really need the money, but because they are not getting the emotional encouragement they need from their husbands to stay with their job of mothering and homemaking.

We can also invest in our spouses by getting out for a date night or getting away for a weekend alone as a couple. A special gift or a dress or inviting your wife on a shopping trip when she least expects it are also good investments. The issue is not what you do; it is that you realize the need to invest in her. This investment is time, first and foremost, and it may also be money. Do not invest your money only in IRAs and retirement plans so you can retire early; by doing so you run the risk of losing the one you would like to retire with, the one you have committed your life to. Why not come home from work a little early tomorrow night, put a fire in the fireplace, grab some hot chocolate, and talk with your wife? Your posterity may be hanging in the balance.

The size of your financial net worth does not mean a thing in this area. Why? Because your greatest *asset*, your wife's love and support, is not listed on the statement. That is why the statements at the beginning of this chapter are true. If you have a good marriage you have everything, regardless of your financial position. The reverse is also true. If you do not have a good marriage, you have failed, even if you are successful at everything else.

We need to spend as much time thinking through our family-investment strategy as we do our retirement-investment strategy. I may receive a greater return in eternity by spending some money on my wife than by buying another stock.

Finally, let's take a bottom-line look at the financial implications of a divided home, which, although bad, are less devastating than the emotional and spiritual losses.

The Financial Implications of Divided Families

If we do not keep our marriages together, not only are there dramatic implications on our posterity and their subsequent spiritual and social capital, but there can also be implications for our financial capital. For example, there's the general rule, "for families with children, breaking into two separate homes increases household costs by about 30 percent."[6]

I remember in the early days of our business I had the opportunity to counsel a young doctor. He made more than a hundred thousand dollars per year, and yet he could not seem to meet all his financial obligations. As we talked he related the difficulty he was having with his two older children. He said he had two daughters, ages fifteen and seventeen, and two sons, ages three and five, so I surmised that he was in a second marriage. Sure enough, as we got into his specific finances, he admitted, "One of my toughest financial obligations is my alimony payment each month." It was also quite costly for him to travel frequently to see his two daughters, who lived with their mother in another city.

This doctor is not alone. In a divorce situation, financial capital is typically dissipated due to the increased cash flow needed to support more than one family. Then when the financial capital is ultimately distributed through the estate, it is very difficult, and in most cases very messy, due to the different families involved. Typically, sorting it all out in the estate plan costs significantly more when there are steprelatives involved. Though the erosion of financial capital is of far less concern than the impact on one's posterity, it is still an issue because God has entrusted us to be stewards of our financial resources.

We need to spend as much time thinking through our family-investment strategy as we do our retirement-investment strategy.

The tendency for our posterity to fail rises when our marriages fall apart, and our children suffer the most. It is difficult for them to marry and raise a family when their model has been shattered. The greatest knowledge they can have is knowing that Mom and Dad are living in harmony. No amount of money can replace a good marriage. This is not a current-yield investment but a future-yield opportunity. The return on our home investment will be revealed clearly in the generations to come through our children and grandchildren. What kind of return will your posterity reveal?

For Further Reflection

1. If you and your wife are both employed outside the home, what would you need to do financially to allow the wife to stay home?

2. Husbands, what ways could you invest financially in your wife?

3. Do your children see a harmonious marriage they would want to emulate?

4. What one thing could you do now to improve your marriage?

13

The Next Generation

The Financial Legacy We Leave to Coming Generations

The glory of young men is their strength,
And the splendor of old men is their gray head.

Proverbs 20:29

The silver-haired head is a crown of glory.

Proverbs 16:31

On a beautiful spring day Grandpa and Grandma pulled into the BMW dealership.

"What color do you think Sara would like the best?" asked Grandpa.

"I don't know," answered Grandma, somewhat reserved. "I know her favorite color is yellow, but I don't know if that would be the best color for a car."

"Yes, I know what you mean," said Grandpa as he rubbed his chin with his hand, pondering what to do. "I think light blue would be a good color for her."

"Yes, light blue would be pretty. But you know, I wonder if we really ought to be doing this for her sixteenth birthday. Don't you think it is a little much?"

"No!" retorted Grandpa. "I think it is just fine. After all, she is a good kid, and you only turn sixteen once."

"You know how frugal her parents are. Don't you think we should at least check it out with them first?"

"No, I don't. It is my money and this is what I want to do. Let's go on into the sales office and get the paperwork started. We don't have all day."

How much should grandparents give the grandchildren? In this chapter, I will try to help you, as a grandparent or a future grandparent, decide what to do. These thoughts come from observing successful grandparents—as well as unsuccessful ones.

The "How Much?" Issue

I am always amazed at grandparents who are unwilling to leave large sums of money to their own children because they were not trained to handle it but will leave significant sums to grandchildren who cannot even talk or walk yet. These grandchildren have yet to be trained in spiritual and social capital, let alone financial stewardship.

I believe this happens for a couple of reasons. First, the tax law encourages what is referred to as "generation skipping." Within the law each grandparent can leave a million dollars in trust to the grandchildren, with the money being available to the grandparent's children during their lifetime. Although available to their children, the money is not taxed in their children's estate at their subsequent death, and their grandchildren receive two million dollars, plus growth with no estate tax erosion.

Second, many grandparents use their money to buy love and acceptance from their grandchildren. They set up trusts or custodial accounts or make large outright gifts to remind the children and grandchildren that they have provided the money for education, a down payment on a home, nice clothes, and the like. They may slip the grandchild a hundred-dollar bill every time they see him or her. The trust funds, custodial accounts, and the money all make the grandparents feel needed and significant in their grandchild's life. Needless to say, these situations can also create a strain between the grandparent and parent.

Any cash gift should only be made to a grandchild after consultation with the parents.

I recommend that, for the most part, grandparents not give cash gifts or assets to their grandchildren either outright or in trust. Instead, this money should go to their adult children (the grandchildren's parents). Even though this recommendation is inconsistent with sophisticated tax-planning techniques such as income shifting and generation skipping, a trust can put grandchildren at a disadvantage. Since their parents have no control over the trust's ultimate distribution to them, the grandchildren could develop a slothful attitude throughout their lives as they wait for the trust to come to them. (If our clients set up generation-skipping trusts we encourage them to name a charity as a potential beneficiary in case the parents feel the trust would be a hindrance if it went to their children—the grandchildren.)

Outright gifts or gifts in custodial accounts can also be harmful. These monies are immediately available to the child, or in the case of custodial accounts, will be available at the age of majority (eighteen or twenty-one, depending on the state). In most cases a young child is better off having too little money than too much. Also, if the parents are teaching the child some fiscal responsibility, the grandparents' gift of a significant sum can undo all the parents seek to accomplish with the child. Suppose the grandchild has lost his baseball glove due to irresponsibility and now has to sacrifice to buy a new one—and then his grandpa hands him two hundred dollars, unannounced.

I feel that *any* cash gift should only be made to a grandchild after consultation with the parents, first to discuss the impact this money can have on the grandchild, and second to agree on the expected use of this money, which can then be discussed with the grandchild. This does not mean grandparents cannot give their grandchildren small cash gifts as they would toys and clothes on birthdays and Christmas. However, you and your children should determine what constitutes a small gift. For some, the allowable limit may be twenty dollars; for others it may be a hundred dollars. Also, the amount may increase with the age of the grandchild. Obviously, the timing of the gifts has some bearing as well. To give a grandchild a hundred dollars on a birthday should pose no big problem, but to give the grandchild a hundred dollars every time the grandparents see the grandchild could be too much.

Also, normal gifts of toys and clothes for Christmas and birthdays should not be excessive and unreasonable. Excessive and unreasonable gifts teach grandchildren to be *consumptive*, creating an expectation that may be hard for them to support when they are on their own.

Is there ever a time to leave significant cash or assets to grandchildren? Yes, cash and/or assets can be left to grandchildren in trust, outright, or in a custodial account for a predetermined purpose if agreed upon by the parent and grandparent. For example, the grandparent could fund the grandchild's college education, as long as the grandchild's parents agree. College education and private school are two areas typically outside the traditional guidelines of parental obligation of support, which include food, shelter, clothing, public schooling, or medical care. I have found that help in these areas is appreciated and typically does not impact the parents' feelings of provision.

A few guidelines about large gifts: First, the grandparents should not constantly remind the parents, grandkids, or others of what they have done. Once they give the gifts they should forget they ever gave them. In some cases, grandparents have used the gifts as leverage to get the parents or grandkids to behave a certain way or do something they want the parents or grandkids to do. The gift thus makes the recipients beholden to the grandparents.

Second, the grandparents' motivation to do something for the grandchildren should never be as punishment to their own children (the grandchildren's parents). This is why giving the money to the parents is better. Do not skip a generation just because you are upset with your children.

Third, if you want to fund your grandchildren's college education, the amount should be such that, with standard assumptions on earnings and education costs, the majority of the funds will be used up by the time the grandchildren finish college. You do not want them to receive a significant amount of money after college or at a later date that might instill complacency and a lack of a work ethic as they wait for the extra funds.

Finally, trusts or custodial accounts for grandchildren should only be funded if the parent (your child) has no need for the funds. It can be very frustrating to a parent to watch significant sums of money accumulate in a child's "education account" while the parent's goals and desires go unmet.

One couple I know would like to build a different house to better meet the needs of their family. To do that now on the husband's income would be difficult. They could benefit from some extra money now, but their parents are making gifts to the three grandchildren for education and bypassing them. There is more than $100,000 in a trust for the education of the grandchildren, and although the parents appreciate this, they are also frustrated that those funds (or some of the funds) are unavailable as a down payment on another house.

In some situations the grandparents do not trust the parents, and as a result they feel they must take care of the grandchildren. This thinking usually creates more problems between the parents and grandparents. This issue brings us full circle: If grandparents did not spend time with their children as they earned the money, those grandparents probably will not be able to leave it in a way that is beneficial to their posterity. Therefore, though some tax benefits can be derived from giving gifts to grandchildren, these benefits are secondary. The most important consideration for grandparents in any gift is the potential impact on the grandchildren and the impact on their relationship with their own children (the parents).

Creative Ways to Use Your Money

Rather than showering grandchildren with money, let me offer some suggestions that are consistent with buying time to develop a godly posterity.

Take the parents and grandchildren on a vacation. Most young couples do not have discretionary funds to take vacations. If the grandparents offer to pay for the trip and include everybody, they invest in a family memory. Not only will a trip together create memories, but the grandparents can spend some time with the grandchildren and reinforce the values and qualities the parents are teaching them. The vacation could be to the lake for a week or to a ski area in Colorado or to a family camp. It could also be as simple as paying for the parents and grandchildren to come for a visit if they live in another state.

Offer to fund private elementary and secondary school. The first ten years of a child's life are the most critical. This is also the time when money may be tightest for the parents. Grandparents may make a strategic investment for the grandchild to attend a private Christian school that could develop godly spiritual and social capital in the grandchild.

Offer to fund housecleaning help. When the parent has young children, something as apparently insignificant as funding a housecleaning service on a regular basis could have an incredible impact on the emotional and physical strength of the mother. This strength can then be channeled into the grandchildren at this formative time in their lives.

Supplement the parents' income so they can get their roles right. In some cases the grandparent could supplement a son or son-in-law's income rather than have the wife go back to work. One son-in-law I know wanted to start a new job, but it would take two years for his income to be at a level where he could support his wife and children without his wife's having to work. So rather than have the daughter go back to work, the grandparents supplemented the son-in-law's income and invested in the family and the grandchildren by enabling the mother to stay at home.

Invest in the grandchildren and their parents by giving of your time. Although it costs the least, perhaps the most important thing grandparents can do is to invest some of their time in the grandchildren and their parents. The ways to do this are numerous. Keep the grandchildren for an afternoon or for a weekend so the parents can get away for a planning session, a marriage seminar, or a retreat. All of these are investments in posterity.

In a society where the extended family is fractured, this investment of time may require your using some resources to rent an apartment close to your children and grandchildren so you can spend some time with them. It may require some funds for airplane tickets to visit more frequently. Or you may drive many hours to spend short amounts of time with them.

Make cash gifts if the extended family is fragmented. As we discussed in Chapter 5, it is more costly today to buy time than it was when the extended family was closer geographically. If you can't be there to give of your time, some unexpected cash could be very welcome to help your children buy time to be with and/or invest in your grandchildren. Remember, it does cost more than when you were raising your children and Grandma was right around the corner.

Undoubtedly, grandparents can think of countless other ways to invest their time and money to enhance the posterity of the two generations that come after them. But remember that posterity is what is important, not trust funds that may leave a legacy of children and grandchildren dependent on the patriarch's wealth.

If you have already set up the trusts, then immediately find a way to develop values and character in your grandchildren. At the same time, do not complicate matters by leaving more to them. Also, if you have skipped a generation, then maybe your children should leave less to their own children from their estate.

Be careful also of your pride. Wanting your children and grandchildren to look a certain way could cause you to overindulge them with material things.

Finally, maximize the time you have left to counsel your children and grandchildren on what it means to be truly successful. A gray head is a wise head, as Proverbs says, and no greater input can be left to the next generations than how to wisely earn and use money.

For Further Reflection

1. Can you recall a situation where cash from grandparents created a sticky situation for you or someone you know? How was the situation handled?

2. If you are a grandparent, have you discussed your estate and your giving plan with your children? Why or why not? Do you think you should?

3. These issues are difficult to discuss in many families. What can you do to open the communication lines in your family?

4. Have these thoughts caused you to reconsider your current estate plan? In what way?

EPILOGUE

A SECOND CHANCE

As Jim Conwell lay motionless on his hospital bed that morning his mind was in a whirl. It was difficult to assimilate all that had happened during the past seventy-two hours. The church . . . Pastor Firnbeck's words about suffering loss . . . the ambulance . . . Jimmy's comments . . . the vivid recollection of the "pile" that grew and grew and was then gone . . . the successful surgery and the realization that he had a second chance.

Although there was a lot to think about, Jim could see it all clearly now. God had let him stare death in the face to give him another chance to add some silver and gold to the pile. It was obvious to him now that his children, Jimmy and Jill, and all those folks from the church were the "precious stones" that would last into eternity and not be burned up.

How could I have been so shortsighted? he thought. *Why have I spent so much time working and ignoring my children? It wasn't intentional. It just sort of happened. Why do I not really care about other people in my life? Why are houses, cars, and country clubs so important to me? Why haven't I spent more time involved with the things of God?* As he pondered these issues, tears of repentance mingled with tears of joy as Jim acknowledged his gratefulness to God for giving him a second chance.

It shouldn't take a brush with death to help us see that the consumption mentality of the seventies and eighties is waning; even the secular world is acknowledging this trend. Shouldn't we, as Christians, be at the forefront of this new thinking? Shouldn't we make the hard decisions regarding our money and our families so we can focus on what lasts into eternity? Isn't it time we became truly prosperous by focusing on leaving a godly posterity?

Jim got a second chance. We may not. After our works are tested by fire will many precious stones, gold, and silver remain (see 1 Cor. 3:12)? That is possible only if we live our lives wisely, and only if we focus on the things that will last forever (our godly posterity) rather than the things that will burn (financial capital), and only if we earn and use our money with a focus on the eternal rather than the temporal.

May we build a legacy that will stand the test of fire!

APPENDIX A

SPIRITUAL ACTION STEPS

Just as certain financial principles relate to our money, certain spiritual principles relate to our spiritual condition. Those principles are:

Spiritual Principle 1: Man is separated from God. The Bible teaches that God loves all men and wants them to know Him. But man is separated from God and His love because of man's sin. The Bible says, "All we like sheep have gone astray; we have turned, every one, to his own way; and the LORD has laid on Him the iniquity of us all" (Isa. 53:6). Paul wrote, "All have sinned and fall short of the glory of God" (Rom. 3:23). You may be thinking that "all" does not include you, but "all" means *all*, and that includes you and me! We are separated from God. This leads us to principle 2.

Spiritual Principle 2: We owe a penalty for our sin. Man is destined to die once, and after this comes judgment (see Heb. 9:27). The Bible also says those who do not know God "shall be punished with everlasting destruction from the presence of the Lord and from the glory of His power" (2 Thess. 1:9). Thus it's clear that we owe a penalty for our sinfulness; the problem is that we are not worthy to pay that penalty. No amount of good works can put us back in right standing with God. There is a solution, however, and it is explained in principle 3.

Spiritual Principle 3: Christ paid the penalty. Romans 5:8 says, "But God demonstrates His own love toward us, in that while we were still sinners, Christ died for us." First Peter 3:18 says, "For Christ also suffered once for sins, the just for the unjust, that He might bring us to God, being put to death in the flesh but made alive by the Spirit." Jesus Christ was born at Christmas to die on Good Friday to pay the penalty for your sins and for mine. He arose from the dead on Easter. It is not enough just to believe these principles; we must go on to principle 4.

Spiritual Principle 4: We must individually accept Christ's payment. We can believe that Christ died for our sins, but if we do not claim that for ourselves through faith we will perish in our sins. Only those who personally receive Jesus Christ into their lives, trusting Him to forgive their sins by faith, can be put in right standing with God and receive the power that only He can give. John 1:12 says, "But as many as received Him, to them He gave the right to become children of God, even to those who believe in His name." In John 5:24 are Jesus' words: "Most assuredly, I say to you, he who hears My word and believes in Him who sent Me has everlasting life, and shall not come into judgment, but has passed from death into life."

How do you claim the reality of Jesus Christ in your life? Very simply, you do it by faith. Jesus says, "Behold, I stand at the door and knock. If anyone hears My voice and opens the door, I will come in to him and dine with him, and he with Me" (Rev. 3:20). If God is knocking on the door of your life, then you need to pray a simple prayer of faith that expresses the desire of your heart. Your prayer can be similar to this: "Lord Jesus, please come into my life and be my Savior and Lord. Please forgive my sins and give me the gift of eternal life. Thank You for forgiving my sins." This prayer, if it expresses the desire of your heart, is the key to opening the door and allowing Christ to come into your life. We know He is there because of this promise:

> And this is the testimony: that God has given us eternal life, and this life is in His Son. He who has the Son has life; he who does not have the Son of God does not have life. These things I have written to you who believe in the name of the Son of God, that you know that you have eternal life, and that you may continue to believe in the name of the Son of God. (1 John 5:11–13)

You can know that you have eternal life if you, by faith, have acknowledged that you are sinful and that Christ paid the penalty for your sins, and if you have asked Him into your heart.

APPENDIX B

BUYING VERSUS RENTING A HOME

Figure B.1 (excerpted from *Money and Your Marriage*) illustrates the cost of renting versus buying homes in different price ranges. Contrary to what one may think, renting is not always a bad situation. For example, in the chart you will see that if you rent a home or apartment for $500 per month, your cash outlay in one year is $6,950 ($6,000 rent plus $600 for utilities and $350 for insurance). While you rent, you keep the $10,000 cash you're saving for a down payment, and you earn $800 in interest on that $10,000; after paying taxes on the $800 interest, you still have earnings of $536. When you subtract the $536 earnings from the $6,950 you paid for rent, utilities, and insurance, you come up with the total cost to you if you rent: $6,414.

But if you look at the "total annual outflow" line on the chart, you will see that if you used the $10,000 to make a down payment on a house, your cash outlay would be greater on an annual basis—anywhere from $7,995 to $13,135, depending on which house you bought. This takes into account the deductibility of the real estate taxes and the interest on the mortgage (noted on the chart on the "tax savings" line). So on a straight annual cash-flow comparison it is less expensive to rent than buy. The positive side of buying, of course, is the potential appreciation on the house. If we assume 10 percent appreciation, we see that the effect on your overall situation is improved if the house can be sold with no real estate commission. However, if the house is sold after one year with a 7 percent real estate commission, you would still have been better off renting (see the line "effect on net worth," where the result is $6,414 for renting compared with $6,500 to $10,605 if you purchased a home).

This analysis points out an interesting fact to consider when trying to decide between buying and renting. In most cases, *you are better off to buy only if you can live in a house for at least two years.* This assumes a sale through a Realtor and no special appreciation factors, such as buying below market, foreclosure, or above-inflation appreciation. *The higher the initial cost of the house, the longer you must live in it to make it cost-effective over renting.* (The annual cost of the house shown on the chart as "Buy #3" is more than double the cost of renting on an annual basis: $6,414 versus $13,135.) If the appreciation of the house is less than 10 percent, you have to live in the home longer to make it pay, from a net-worth standpoint. Of course, the opposite is also true. If you encounter runaway inflation and the house appreciates more than 10 percent, it will become less costly than renting.

You should take into account your occupation and your lifestyle needs and goals before you decide to rent or buy. From a strictly financial viewpoint, as our analysis has shown, you will be better off renting rather than buying if your vocation is one that requires relocation every two to three years. If you are uncertain when vocational changes may occur or if they are likely to occur more infrequently than every two or three years, then buying will make more financial sense.

Vocational and financial considerations aside, there may be other reasons for buying as opposed to renting. Even if you live in a home for only a short time, the responsibilities and satisfaction that can come from owning rather than renting may override your potential financial costs. You may find that your desire for domestic home duties—such as mowing the yard and decorating, among others—is only met through home ownership, and you are willing to incur additional costs.

The key to this decision is your evaluating the purchase of a home with a proper perspective on the real cost, both financially and emotionally, all the while realizing the underlying need to live within your income. Stretching budgets may make sense to the world, but the potential risk to the marriage and time with your posterity is not worth it. If you buy when you cannot afford to buy (stretching beyond your income and depleting all emergency funds), then the home becomes a burden. If marital harmony and time margin is what you want, do not allow a house to disrupt it. Buying a home may be the American dream, but use wisdom in deciding whether it is best for you at your current station in life.

HOUSING
Illustration: Buying vs. Renting

	Rent	Buy #1	Buy #2	Buy #3	
Cost of Home:	-0-	$65,000	$86,000	$110,000	___
Expenses:					
Mortgage payment	-0-	6,000	8,400	11,000	___
Rent payment	6,000	-0-	-0-	-0-	___
Utilities	600	1,200	1,500	1,800	___
Taxes	-0-	800	900	1,000	___
Insurance	350	500	600	700	___
Repairs/ maintenance	-0-	400	500	600	___
Closing costs	-0-	1,000	1,250	1,500	___
Tax savings	-0-	(1,905)	(2,752)	(3,465)	___
Total annual outflow	($6,950)	($7,995)	($10,398)	($13,135)	
Gain:					
Appreciation	-0-	$6,500	$8,600	$11,000	___
Interest income (net of tax)	$536	-0-	-0-	-0-	-0-
Effect on net worth	(6,414)	(1,495)	(1,793)	(2,135)	
Effect on net worth with 7% commission on sale		(6,500)	(8,420)	(10,605)	

Assumptions:

Facts: $10,000 down; 10.5% interest on 30-year mortgage; 33% tax bracket (28% Fed and 5% state)

Appreciation is calculated at 10% of sales price.

Interest income is calculated at 8%.

Assume 7% Realtor fee if sold.

FIGURE B.1

APPENDIX C

FINANCIAL ACTION STEPS

By design this book is a "why-to" book rather than a "how-to" book. It attempts to provide you with a new way of thinking about your money and your family, rather than to give you a number of specifics on handling your money. It also is designed to provide you with a philosophical base for your decisions concerning your money, your job, and your children.

But now that you know *why* it's important to deal correctly with your money, what should you do specifically? The purpose of this appendix is to highlight briefly some specific steps you can take and to point you to some resources that will help you with these steps.

STEP ONE: IMPLEMENT A CASH-FLOW CONTROL SYSTEM

I recently heard an interesting story regarding bill-paying. A woman stacked all her bills on her desk and then paid them by starting with the top bill and working her way down through the stack. She would pay until she ran out of money, then she wouldn't pay any more bills that month. She moved the remaining bills to the top of the stack and started over the next month. When one of her creditors contacted her about getting paid late or, in some months, not at all, the woman responded, "Sir, if you don't quit bugging me, I won't even put your bill in the stack!"

Without a doubt, the most important step any family can take to make money a nonissue (and thus be able to focus mental and emotional energy on raising a godly posterity) is to implement a cash-flow control system. This system ensures that the family will live within the amount allotted for living expenses and, as a result, not spend more than they are making. Spending less than you make is the critical step in achieving financial freedom and being able to achieve balance in life.

To begin the process of setting up a cash-flow control system, two steps must be taken. First, you should work through the following schedule to determine how much money you have available for living expenses.

Income	___________
less taxes	___________
less giving	___________
= Amount left for living expenses	___________

Second, once you have the amount available for living expenses, allocate it to appropriate budget categories (see the Living Expenses worksheet, fig. C.1). Once the available amount has been allocated to the various categories you are ready to implement a system. (Note: Not all the available money should be allocated; leave some for savings.)

LIVING EXPENSES

Date:________________________

	Amount Paid Monthly	Amount Paid Other Than Monthly	Total Annual Amount
Housing			
Mortgage/Rent	$_______	$_______	$_______
Insurance	_______	_______	_______
Property Taxes	_______	_______	_______
Electricity	_______	_______	_______
Heating	_______	_______	_______
Water	_______	_______	_______
Sanitation	_______	_______	_______
Telephone	_______	_______	_______
Cleaning	_______	_______	_______
Repairs/Maint.	_______	_______	_______
Supplies	_______	_______	_______
Other	_______	_______	_______
Total*	**$_______**	**$_______**	**$_______**
Food*	**$_______**	**$_______**	**$_______**
Clothing*	**$_______**	**$_______**	**$_______**
Transportation			
Insurance	_______	_______	_______
Gas and Oil	_______	_______	_______
Repairs/Maint.	_______	_______	_______
Parking	_______	_______	_______
Other	_______	_______	_______
Total*	**$_______**	**$_______**	**$_______**
Entertainment/Recreation			
Eating Out	_______	_______	_______
Baby-sitters	_______	_______	_______
Mags./Newspapers	_______	_______	_______
Vacation	_______	_______	_______
Clubs/Activities	_______	_______	_______
Other	_______	_______	_______
Total*	**$_______**	**$_______**	**$_______**
Insurance			
Life	_______	_______	_______
Disability	_______	_______	_______
Other	_______	_______	_______
Total*	**$_______**	**$_______**	**$_______**

FIGURE C.1

LIVING EXPENSES (cont.)

	Amount Paid Monthly	Amount Paid Other Than Monthly	Total Annual Amount
Medical Expenses			
Insurance	$______	$______	$______
Doctors	______	______	______
Dentists	______	______	______
Drugs	______	______	______
Total*	**$______**	**$______**	**$______**
Children			
School Lunches	$______	$______	$______
Allowances	______	______	______
Tuition	______	______	______
Lessons	______	______	______
Other	______	______	______
Total*	**$______**	**$______**	**$______**
Gifts			
Christmas	$______	$______	$______
Birthdays	______	______	______
Anniversary	______	______	______
Other	______	______	______
Total*	**$______**	**$______**	**$______**
Miscellaneous			
Toiletries	$______	$______	$______
Husband: misc.	______	______	______
Wife: misc.	______	______	______
Clng./Laundry	______	______	______
Animal Care	______	______	______
Beauty/Barber	______	______	______
Other	______	______	______
Other	______	______	______
Total*	**$______**	**$______**	**$______**
Total Living Expenses	**$______**	**$______**	**$______**

FIGURE C.1 (cont.)

To describe it "in a nutshell," the control system works like this: Take the amount allocated for each budget category and put it in an envelope and spend until it is gone. Once it's gone you cannot spend any more in that category until the next month unless you get the money out of another envelope.

Needless to say, the "envelope system" of cash-flow control sounds old-fashioned and trite. But in theory all cash-flow control systems work this way. They include allocating a predetermined amount and a way to monitor how you are doing with your spending relative to that amount. Many individuals tell me they are on a budget, but when I ask how their budget works, they say, "Well, I keep track of what I spend each month and total it up." This is not a cash-flow control system. Tracking what you spend will help you learn how much you need to allocate to a category, such as food, but it does not help you control it.

Each month Julie has five hundred dollars for food. Our system allows her to know how she is doing against the budgeted amount of five hundred dollars at any point during the month. This is the essence of a cash-flow control system. If she just totalled up what she spent each month, she would have no way to ensure she is within the five hundred dollars—until it was too late.

To help you in this area I would highly recommend any of the following resources:

- Ron Blue's booklet, "How to Control Your Cash Flow." To learn how to order, send a written request for the materials catalog to Ronald Blue and Company, 1100 Johnson Ferry Road, Suite 600, Atlanta, Georgia 30342.

- Ron Blue's book, *Master Your Money* (Thomas Nelson, 1986).
- Larry Burkett's *Financial Planning Workbook: A Family Budgeting Guide* (Moody Press, 1979 and 1990).
- Russ Crosson's *Money and Your Marriage* (Word, 1989). See, in particular, chapter 9. To learn how to order, send a written request for the materials catalog to Ronald Blue and Company, 1100 Johnson Ferry Road, Suite 600, Atlanta, Georgia 30342.

It may take twelve to eighteen months to implement a system that will work for your family, but the resulting freedom and lack of anxiety is worth the investment of time.

Step Two: Implement a Sequential Investment Strategy

Most people think investments are glamorous. They think if they could make a big yield on their investments, they would have it made; they would not have to work so hard, and all their financial problems would go away. The truth is that people accumulate financial wealth by spending less than they make over a long period of time and preserving capital with their investments. They do not accumulate financial wealth through investments only. Financial wealth is a by-product for those who do not seek it. It is a by-product of working hard and spending less than they make (cash-flow control) and then investing conservatively so they do not lose the capital they have accumulated.

And anyway, as we have discussed in this book, work is a positive thing, not a negative factor. Our children should learn a work ethic—and see it modeled in us. Thus, a critical action step is to implement a sound investment strategy that will promote—and not detract—from the development of a godly posterity. A sequential investment strategy for preserving accumulated capital is outlined below:

Step 1: Eliminate all short-term, high-interest debt such as credit cards and consumer debts on such items as furniture, cars, and appliances.

Step 2: Set aside three to six months' living expenses in a savings account or a money-market fund for emergencies. Although this type of investment will only earn the prevailing money-market rates of interest, by having the emergency fund you will avoid having to pay for emergencies on a credit card and as a result you will avoid paying the high interest rates charged for credit-card debt.

Step 3: In an interest-bearing savings account or a money-market fund, save money for planned purchases of major items such as a down payment for a house, or for automobiles, furniture, and the like. You will only earn the prevailing money-market rates of interest, but you will avoid the heavy charges that occur if you need to finance a car or furniture.

Step 4: Accumulate funds to meet long-term goals. When you reach this step you are ready to invest, in the traditional sense of the word. At this point you should seek expert advice to develop a diversified investment plan in keeping with your goals, temperament, income, tax bracket, and age. Any plan should include fixed-income investments such as bonds, treasury notes, and certificates of deposit, as well as equities (stocks) and real estate.

As a practical suggestion I recommend that if you are involved in steps 1 through 3 and need some help with determining the best money-market funds and savings accounts, you consider Austin Pryor's fine monthly newsletter: *Sound Mind Investing*, published by Austin Pryor and Associates. For information about subscribing, write to:

Sound Mind Investing
P.O. Box 22128
Louisville, Kentucky 40252-9985

I would also recommend as a resource Arthur Pryor's book by the same name, which was published in 1993 by Moody Press.

If you are at step 4 and have a surplus of funds for investment, either personally or in a retirement plan, I would recommend contacting Ronald Blue and Company at 1100 Johnson Ferry Road, Suite 600, Atlanta, Georgia 30342. You could also contact your local broker, but be sure to request a professionally managed approach (using several money managers in different asset classes) to the management of your money.

I would also recommend the following as good resources to better understand investments:

- Larry Burkett, *Investing for the Future* (Victor Books, 1992).
- Ron Blue, "How to Determine Your Investment Strategy" (a booklet). To learn how to order, send a written request for the materials catalog to Ronald Blue and Company, 1100 Johnson Ferry Road, Suite 600, Atlanta, Georgia 30342.

Step Three: Make Sure You Have the Correct Amount of Life Insurance

A third action step is to ensure there is adequate life insurance. In the early years of my business a young man explained to me that he did not really think life insurance was necessary. He thought God would meet the needs of his wife and children; buying life insurance, he believed, was in some way admitting a lack of faith. I asked him what would happen to his wife and two children if something happened to him.

He explained that either the church would take care of them, the government would provide for them through welfare, or his wife would have to work. Although any of these options was a possibility, I explained that the best alternative might be to have some life insurance to ensure that his wife would not be dependent on the government, and so that, if the church did not meet her needs, she would not have to go back to work. In essence, the life insurance was an investment in his posterity, so his wife could stay home and impact his posterity (see Chapter 12).

That's why adequate life insurance is so important. It provides a sum of money that makes it possible for the wife (in the case of the husband's death) to continue to be a stay-at-home mom and impact their posterity. A smaller amount of life insurance in the event of the wife's death gives the husband some flexibility to spend time with the children during the transition and also enables him to hire some nanny-type help.

The Life Insurance Needs Analysis Worksheet (fig. C.2) is designed to help you determine the amount of insurance you need at your current station in life. The key concept here is "current station in life." Typically, the need for insurance will be reduced as children are educated and leave home.

LIFE INSURANCE NEEDS ANALYSIS WORKSHEET*

Income Goals for the Family	
Living Expenses [1]	________________
Taxes	________________
Giving	________________
Total Income Needed	________________ **A**
Sources of Income [2]	
Social Security	________________
Pension or Retirement Plans	________________
Annuities or Trusts	________________
Investment Income [3]	________________
Spouse Working	________________
Other	________________
	________________
Total Income Available	________________ **B**
Additional Income Needed (per year) [4]	________________ **A - B = C**
Insurance Required to Provide Income [5] (Additional Income Needed x 10) (current need)	________________ **C x 10 = D**
Additional Funds Needed for:	
Funeral Costs	________________
Debt Repayment (current need)	________________
Estate Tax and Settlement Expense (long-term need)	________________
Education Costs (current need)	________________
Major Purchases	________________
________________	________________
________________	________________
Total Additional Funds Needed	________________ **E**
Insurance Needed [6]	________________ **E + D = F**

FIGURE C.2

LIFE INSURANCE NEEDS ANALYSIS WORKSHEET (cont.)*

Assets Available for Sale:	
Real Estate	________________
Stocks, Bonds	________________
Savings Available (to meet needs listed above) (7)	________________
________________	________________
________________	________________
________________	________________
Total from Sale of Assets	________________ **G**
Total Insurance Needed (8)	________________ **F - G = H**
Insurance Available Now	________________ **I**
Additional Insurance Needed	________________ **H - I = K**

Notes:

(1) Use 80% of present annual living expense.
(2) Income anticipated on a regular basis.
(3) Income from investments not liquidated.
(4) The Total Income Needed less the Total Income Available (A - B = C).
(5) This assumes the life insurance proceeds could be invested at 10% and provide the needed amounts. The investment percentage may be contingent on economic conditions or investment knowledge. The multiplication factor is 1 divided by the percentage return on insurance proceeds.
Example: 10% = 1/.10 = 10; 8% = 1/.08 = 12.5; 12% = 1/.12 = 8.33
(6) Insurance needed is the sum of insurance to provide income (D) plus additional funds needed (E).
(7) Savings available would be only that part of savings that could be applied to meet the needs listed above. It would not include the savings needed to meet family living goals.
(8) Total insurance needed is the insurance needed less the amount available from the sale of assets (F - G = H).

NOTE: No adjustment has been made in these calculations for inflation. If you feel that you can earn 10% but that will be eroded by 3–4% inflation, then you should use 6–7% in Step 5 and not 10%. This will increase the amount of insurance needed. You can use any investment or inflation assumption you would like.

**How to Plan Your Life Insurance Program (Atlanta: Ronald Blue and Co., 1987) 18–19.*

FIGURE C.2 (cont.)

Most couples are underinsured when they need to be insured (early in their marriage when they need money to spend time with and educate their posterity) and overinsured when they do not need it (later in their marriage when life insurance proceeds compound estate problems by leaving too much to the children).

You must seriously analyze your life insurance situation frequently enough (every two to three years) to ensure that the amount you have is adequate for what you are trying to do with your posterity but not so great that it would hinder what you are trying to do.

To understand life insurance better and to determine the company you should use and the type of life insurance you need, I would recommend the "Special Ratings Issue" of the Insurance Forum published each March/April and September/October by:

Insurance Forum, Inc.
P.O. Box 245
Ellettsville, IN 47429

Step Four: Go See Your Attorney and Have Wills Drafted

Another action step you must take sooner than later is to have an estate attorney draft a will for you and your spouse. This may cost from a few hundred dollars on up, but it is a necessary investment if you want your financial capital to pass to your heirs the way you want it to.

I would be careful in this area not to try to save a few dollars. You do not want to be "penny-wise and pound-foolish" when it comes to how you leave your assets. Some individuals just copy another person's documents, only changing the names. Others have just done handwritten wills. State and national estate laws are so complex it seems prudent to go to an attorney who is qualified in your state's estate laws to have these wills drafted.

To understand the specifics of wills and to better communicate with the attorney, I recommend the following resources:

- David W. Belin, *Leaving Money Wisely* (Scribner's Sons/MacMillan Publishing, 1990).
- Ron Blue, "Principles and Techniques of Estate Planning" (a booklet). To learn how to order, send a written request for the materials catalog to Ronald Blue and Company, 1100 Johnson Ferry Road, Suite 600, Atlanta, Georgia 30342.
- Ron Blue, *Master Your Money* (Thomas Nelson, 1986).
- Robert A. Esperti and Renno L. Petersa, *Living Trust* (Penguin, 1988).
- Stephan R. Leimberg, Stephen N. Kandell, Herbert L. Levy, Ralph Gano Miller, and Morey S. Rosenbloom, *The Tools and Techniques of Estate Planning* (The National Underwriter Company, Cincinnati, 1990).
- Paul J. Lochray, *The Financial Planner's Guide to Estate Planning* (Prentice-Hall, 1987).

Endnotes

Chapter 1 A Glimpse of Eternity

1. This hypothetical story was written by Pat Harley to communicate the author's key points.

2. Bill Richards, "Dear Mother Teresa, How Are You Fixed for Cash Just Now?" *Wall Street Journal*.

3. Randy Alcorn, *Money, Possessions, and Eternity* (Wheaton, Ill.: Tyndale, 1989), 59.

Chapter 2 Prosperity

1. Rosalie J. Slater, *American Dictionary of the English Language* (San Francisco: Foundation for American Christian Education, 1967), 9–11. It is also interesting to note that Webster's dictionary flowed from his desire to establish for the infant country of America a common language consistent with its constitutional course. He knew that political separation from the Old World would not be enough to sustain this young republic if it did not also separate itself philosophically and educationally. Thus, a language was necessary for America that would avoid the corruption, folly, tyranny, and vices of Europe. Webster believed it should also promote virtue and patriotism and embellish and improve the sciences.

2. Paul Lee Tan, *Encyclopedia of 7700 Illustrations* (Rockville, Md.: Assurance Publishers, 1979), 802.

3. Matthew Henry, *Commentary on the Whole Bible* (Grand Rapids, Mich.: Zondervan, 1961), 794–95.

4. Dennis Haack, "Which Success Really Counts?" *Moody Monthly*, March 1990.

5. Tan, *Encyclopedia of 7700 Illustrations*, 1374.

6. Haack, "Which Success Really Counts?"

7. Rob Phillips, "Beyond Success," *Sky*, November 1992, 18–22.

Chapter 3 Posterity

1. Additional verses on posterity include Psalm 103:17–18; Psalm 34:16; Exodus 20:5–6; Deuteronomy 7:9; Isaiah 59:21; and Isaiah 66:22.

Chapter 4 The Life-Overview Balance Sheet

1. William R. Mattox, Jr., "The Family-Friendly Corporation, Strengthening the Ties that Bind," *Family Policy*, November 1992, 3.

2. Tan, *Encyclopedia of 7700 Illustrations*, 802.

Chapter 5 The Principle of Time Replacement

1. Charles R. Swindoll, *Living on the Ragged Edge* (Waco, Tx.: Word, 1985), 68.

2. Leon A. Danco, *Beyond Survival* (Reston, Va.: Reston Publishing, 1975), 178.

3. "How Americans Are Running Out of Time," *Time*, 24 April 1989, 74–76.

4. Richard A. Swenson, M.D., *Margin* (Colorado Springs, Colo.: NavPress, 1992), 116.

5. Ibid., 15, 30.

6. Gil Schwartz, "Making the Case for Taking a Break," *Fortune*, 9 March 1992, 155.

7. Jeremy Rifkin, *Time Wars* (New York: Simon and Schuster, 1987), 59.

8. James Dobson, *Focus on the Family Newsletter*, December 1992, 1–2.

9. Dr. Patrick T. Malone, "Heavy Stress Drives Motorists to Take Hostility on the Road," *Atlanta Journal and Constitution*.

10. Swenson, *Margin*, 88.

11. Essay from Life Messengers, 1926 Densmore Ave. N., Seattle, Washington 98133. Used by permission.

12. E. F. Schumacher, *Good Work* (New York: Simon and Schuster, 1987), 25.

13. Jeff Davidson, "A Father's Blessing," *Focus on the Family Magazine*, June 1986. Used by permission.

Chapter 6 A New Understanding of Our Work

1. Billy Graham, quoted in *Atlanta Journal and Constitution*, 17 August 1992.
2. Jane Fonda, quoted in *World Magazine*, 23 May 1992.
3. Pete Petit, quoted in *Delta In-Flight Magazine*.
4. Jim Henderson, "Lynch Quits While He's at the Top," *USA Today*, 29 March 1990.
5. Marjie McGraw, "A new world according to Garth," *First* magazine, 28 June 1993, 31.
6. Dan Stamp, quoted by Mark Stevens in "Workaholics Should Find Time to Enjoy Life," *Atlanta Journal and Constitution*, 15 May 1989.
7. Brandon Tartikoff, quoted in "Men Alter Priorities for Home Life's Sake," *Atlanta Journal and Constitution*, 2 November 1992.
8. Jeffrey A. Tannenbaum, "Entrepreneurs and Second Acts," *Wall Street Journal*.
9. William Johnston, quoted by Susan Dentzer in "How We Will Live," *U.S. News & World Report*, 25 December 1989.
10. Mattox, *Family Policy*.
11. Lesley Alderman, *Money*, December 1991, 75.
12. C. H. Spurgeon, *The Treasury of David* (McLean, Va.: MacDonald, n.d.), 88.
13. Phillips, "Beyond Success," 22.
14. Ibid.

Chapter 7 Wanting It All

1. Carrie Teegardin, "Load Too Heavy for Many," *Atlanta Journal and Constitution*, 6 September 1992.
2. Ibid.